Living in China

PHOTOS RETO GUNTLI   TEXT DAISANN MCLANE

LIVING IN CHINA

EDITED BY / HERAUSGEGEBEN VON / SOUS LA DIRECTION DE

ANGELIKA TASCHEN

TASCHEN

HONG KONG KÖLN LONDON LOS ANGELES MADRID PARIS TOKYO

Contents / Inhalt / Sommaire

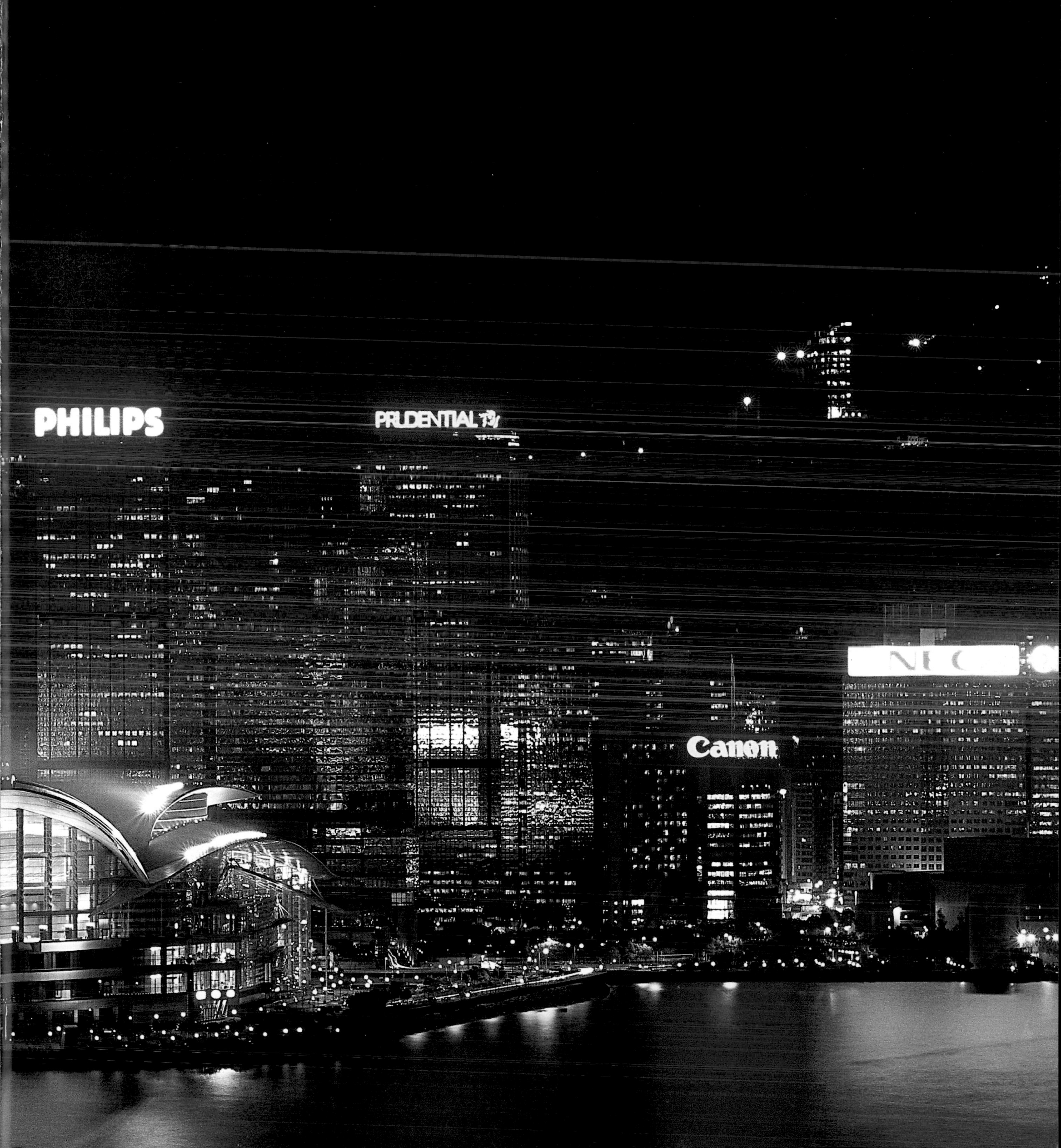
PHILIPS
PRUDENTIAL
Canon
NEC

DAVID TANG

HONG KONG

Some say a man's home is his castle, but David Tang's eclectic, eccentric house is more like a playground – for the mind as well as the senses. Hong Kong's most famous *bon vivant* businessman and art collector lives with his wife in one of the city's rare historic houses, located on a winding road in the hills above the skyscraper-mad city. Unusually for Hong Kong, the rooms have high ceilings and rectangular and square spaces. "I have lived there for years and I would never want to leave," Tang declares. Every space is filled with a profusion of the things Tang loves best in life – plush chairs (each one flanked by a reading lamp), fine contemporary and old paintings, his nine-foot Steinway grand piano, and piles upon piles of books.

The sitting room with its intense greens and reds and vibrant fuschias reflects the aesthetic of his Hong Kong boutique Shanghai Tang. "I hate Minimalism. Rooms look their best when they are covered with colours and objects." By contrast, the bedroom – where Tang retires early to read voraciously – is a muted haven of pale hues, presided over by Chinese scrolls that read: "A palace of quietude and calm discussions; with poets reading poems in serenity."

David Tang, Geschäftsmann, Bonvivant und Kunstsammler, lebt zusammen mit seiner Frau in einem historischen Haus, wie es in Hongkong nicht mehr viele gibt. Das Haus liegt in den Hügeln hoch über den Wolkenkratzern der Stadt und hat ungewöhnlich hohe Räume. Tang: „In all den Jahren, in denen ich hier lebe, wollte ich noch nie wegziehen." Tang mag Opulentes. Jeder Raum ist gefüllt mit üppig gepolsterten, von Lampen flankierten Sesseln, wertvollen Bildern, einem großen Steinway-Flügel und Büchern.

Die Farben im Wohnzimmer, Grün, Rot und ein leuchtendes Fuchsia, sind auch die Hausfarben seiner Boutique Shanghai Tang: „Minimalismus ist nicht mein Ding. Die Kombination von unterschiedlichen Dingen und bunte Farben sind eine effektvolle Kombination, wie man bei allen großartigen Palästen und Häusern dieser Welt sieht." Einzig sein Schlafzimmer ist in zurückhaltenden Farbtönen gehalten. Hier zieht er sich oft früh am Abend zurück, um zu lesen. Auf einer chinesischen Hängerolle steht: „Ein Palast des Friedens und der ruhigen Gespräche, mit Dichtern, die Gedichte mit klarem Geist vortragen."

Si la demeure d'un homme est son chateau celle de David Tang serait plutôt un terrain de jeux. L'homme d'affaires et collectionneur, le plus célèbre bon vivant de Hong-Kong, vit avec son épouse dans l'une des dernières maisons historiques de la ville, dans une rue sinueuse qui domine les gratte-ciels. Les pièces sont hautes sous plafond, détail inhabituel à Hong-Kong. « J'habite ici depuis des années et ne voudrais vivre nulle part ailleurs », déclare Tang. L'intérieur est rempli d'une profusion de tout ce qui fait son bonheur : profonds fauteuils (flanqués d'une lampe), tableaux contemporains et anciens, son Steinway à queue et des piles de livres.

Le salon vert, rouge et fuchsia reflète l'esthétique de sa boutique Shanghai Tang. « Je hais le minimalisme. J'ai remarqué que, dans tous les palaces et les grandes demeures, les pièces sont plus belles remplies de couleurs et d'objets. » En revanche, la chambre, où il se retire tôt pour dévorer des livres, est un havre de tons pâles dominé par un rouleau chinois proclamant : « Un palais de quiétude et de discussions calmes ; où les poètes lisent des poèmes dans la sérénité. »

LEFT ABOVE:
View of Tang's garden through the arch of his historic house, and his custom-made "Dragon" bicycle.

LEFT BELOW:
French windows lead to a balcony piled high with old Italian silk cushions.

RIGHT:
In the foyer, blue silk draperies and a blue antique rug from Tibet.

LINKS OBEN:
Blick auf den Garten durch den Torbogen des historischen Hauses und auf Tangs maßgefertigtes „Dragon"-Fahrrad.

LINKS UNTEN:
Große Flügelfenster führen auf einen Balkon, auf dem antike italienische Seidenkissen liegen.

RECHTE SEITE:
Eingangshalle mit blauen Seidenvorhängen und blauem antikem Tibet-Teppich.

EN HAUT À GAUCHE :
Le jardin, vu depuis l'arche de la maison historique, et la bicyclette « dragon » de Tang, fabriquée sur mesure.

EN BAS À GAUCHE :
Les portes-fenêtres s'ouvrent sur un balcon où sont empilés des coussins en soie italienne ancienne.

PAGE DE DROITE :
Dans le vestibule, la note bleue des draperies en soie et d'un tapis tibétain ancien.

DAVID TANG / HONG KONG

The sitting room has a
nine-foot Steinway piano,
and a red velvet lounger
Tang rescued from a Paris
hotel.

Das Wohnzimmer mit dem
knapp drei Meter langen
Steinway-Flügel und dem
roten, runden Samtsofa,
das Tang aus einem Pariser
Hotel gerettet hat.

Dans le salon, un piano à
queue Steinway de 3 m
de long et une banquette
ronde en velours rouge
provenant d'un hôtel
parisien.

12

DAVID TANG / HONG KONG

LEFT ABOVE:
Another view of the sitting room; every chair has its own reading lamp.

LEFT BELOW:
Brightly colored walls set off Tang's collection of paintings by Jack Vettriano, Augustus John, and Douglas Gray.

RIGHT ABOVE:
Sitting room. The acid-green armchair and embroidered orange-red velvet curtains display Tang's preference for bold, intense colors and his love of rich detail.

RIGHT BELOW:
Every space is filled with paintings from Tang's eclectic collection.

LINKE SEITE OBEN:
Jeder Sessel im Wohnzimmer hat seine eigene Leselampe.

LINKE SEITE UNTEN:
Auf den farbigen Wänden kommen die Werke von Jack Vettriano, Augustus John und Douglas Gray aus Tangs Kunstsammlung besonders gut zur Geltung.

RECHTS OBEN:
Die giftgrünen Sessel und bestickten orangeroten Samtvorhänge im Wohnzimmer offenbaren Tangs Vorliebe für kräftige, intensive Farben und seinen Hang zu prunkvollen Elementen.

RECHTS UNTEN:
Die Bilder aus Tangs eklektischer Sammlung füllen jeden Raum.

PAGE DE GAUCHE, EN HAUT :
Une autre vue du salon ; chaque siège a sa propre lampe de lecture.

PAGE DE GAUCHE, EN BAS :
Les couleurs vives des murs mettent en valeur la collection d'œuvres d'art signées Jack Vettriano, Augustus John et Douglas Gray.

EN HAUT À DROITE :
Le salon. Le fauteuil vert acidulé et les rideaux brodés en velours rouge orangé témoignent du goût de Tang pour les couleurs fortes et intenses, ainsi que de son amour des détails raffinés.

EN BAS À DROITE :
La collection éclectique de tableaux occupe le moindre espace.

DAVID TANG / HONG KONG

LEFT PAGE:
Tang's huge collection of books spills over to his dining room. The setting is completed by two large paintings in unusual, oval-shaped wooden frames.

RIGHT PAGE:
Tang's serene, neutral-toned bedroom with traditional Chinese scrolls that read: "A palace of quietude and calm discussions; with poets reading poems in serenity."

LINKE SEITE:
Im Esszimmer stapeln sich Bücher aus David Tangs umfangreicher Sammlung. Die Szenerie wird durch zwei große Gemälde in ungewöhnlichen, ovalen Holzrahmen ergänzt.

RECHTE SEITE:
Tangs friedvolles Schlaf-zimmer in neutralen Farb-tönen und mit traditionellen chinesischen Hängerollen. „Ein Palast des Friedens und der ruhigen Gespräche, mit Dichtern, die Gedichte mit klarem Geist vor-tragen."

PAGE DE GAUCHE :
L'impressionnante collection de livres déborde dans la salle à manger. Le décor est complété par deux grandes peintures dans d'originaux cadres en bois ovales.

PAGE DE DROITE :
La chambre à coucher de Tang, avec ses tons neutres et ses rouleaux traditionnels chinois où il est écrit : « Un palais de quiétude et de discussions calmes ; où les poètes lisent des poèmes dans la sérénité. »

BAMBOO WALL

COMMUNE BY THE GREAT WALL, BADALING

China's Great Wall, constructed between the 5th century BC and the 16th century, was an architectural response to an ancient challenge – the threat of invasion. The Commune by the Great Wall, built in 2002, represents a more modern challenge. First, each of the 12 architects commissioned for the project had to design a modern house that could stand in the shadow of one of the world's most enduring landmarks. And then, they had to build it for just one million dollars, using Chinese construction materials. The result? Some of the finest avant-garde Asian architecture around.

Japanese architect Kengo Kuma's Bamboo Wall pays homage to Asia's most versatile and evocative building material. Bamboo's lightness makes a perfect counterpoint to the solidity of the Great Wall (the project is located 70 km north of Beijing). Moveable bamboo walls line the façade, affording open views of the wild countryside. Guests who stay here (the Commune is part of a Kempinski hotel) can wander among six bedrooms, two indoor stone bridges, and a tea room. At night, you can spot the lights from a Great Wall tower shining through the slats.

Die Chinesische Mauer wurde zwischen dem 5. Jahrhundert v. Chr. und dem 16. Jahrhundert erbaut. Sie diente als Schutzwall gegen nördliche Grenzvölker. 2002 erhielt das Weltwunder eine würdige Ergänzung: die Commune by the Great Wall an der Großen Mauer in Badaling, 70 km nördlich von Peking. Ein Dutzend Architekten, die in Asien bauen, erhielten den Auftrag, je ein Haus zu entwerfen, das visuell mit der Großen Mauer harmoniert, aus chinesischen Baumaterialien besteht und nicht mehr als eine Million Dollar kostet. Entstanden ist ein außergewöhnlicher Komplex asiatischer Avantgarde-Architektur.

Das Bamboo Wall, das Werk des japanischen Architekten Kengo Kuma, ist eine Hommage an den Bambus, dem wohl typischsten Baumaterial für Asien. Seine Leichtigkeit bildet einen Kontrast zur massiven Großen Mauer. So umzäunen Bambus-Schiebewände, die einen Blick auf die unberührte Landschaft erlauben, das Haus. Das Bamboo Wall und die anderen elf Architekturjuwelen gehören zur Kempinski-Hotelgruppe. Die Gäste können zwischen sechs Schlafzimmern und einem Teesalon umherwandeln.

La Grande Muraille de Chine fut la réponse architecturale à un vieux défi : les invasions mongoles. Inaugurée en 2002, la Commune by the Great Wall relève un défi plus moderne. 12 architectes furent chargés de construire une maison moderne capable de cohabiter avec l'un des monuments les plus célèbres du monde. Chacun disposait d'un budget d'un million de dollars et devait utiliser des matériaux chinois. Le résultat ? Un complexe d'habitations digne d'un musée des fleurons de l'architecture asiatique d'avant-garde.

La réalisation du japonais Kengo Kuma rend hommage au matériau le plus polyvalent et évocateur d'Asie. La légèreté du bambou en fait le parfait contrepoint à la masse solide de la Grande Muraille (la maison se dresse près du tronçon de Badaling, à 70 km au nord de Pékin). Les cloisons amovibles de la façade offrent des vues dégagées sur la campagne. Comme les onze autres projets initiaux, Bamboo Wall appartient au groupe hôtelier Kempinski et compte six chambres, deux passerelles intérieures en pierre et un salon de thé. La nuit, on aperçoit les lumières d'une tour de guet entre les bambous.

LEFT ABOVE:
Moveable bamboo walls enclose the house from all sides and create a rustic feeling.

LEFT BELOW:
Large plate-glass windows in the dining room link the exterior bamboo walls with the ones within.

RIGHT ABOVE:
The nearby section of China's Great Wall sees few tourists. You can walk alone for miles.

RIGHT BELOW:
Sunshine streaming through tall bamboo lends serenity to all the interior spaces.

LINKE SEITE OBEN:
Die verschiebbaren Bambuswände schließen das Haus von allen Seiten ab.

LINKE SEITE UNTEN:
Große Wandfenster im Esszimmer machen aus den Bambuswänden innen und außen optisch eine Einheit.

RECHTS OBEN:
Kaum Touristen: An diesem Teil der Großen Mauer kann man kilometerlang spazieren, ohne einer Seele zu begegnen.

RECHTS UNTEN:
Meditatives Lichtspiel zwischen den Bambusstäben sorgt für eine friedliche Atmosphäre in allen Räumen.

PAGE DE GAUCHE, EN HAUT :
Des cloisons amovibles en bambou ceignent la maison et lui donnent une allure rustique.

PAGE DE GAUCHE, EN BAS :
Dans la salle à manger, les grandes baies vitrées unissent les cloisons en bambou de l'extérieur et celles de l'intérieur.

À DROITE, EN HAUT :
Cette portion de la Grande Muraille est peu fréquentée par les touristes. On peut marcher des heures sans voir personne.

À DROITE, EN BAS :
Les rayons obliques du soleil entre les hauts bambous dorment aux pièces une atmosphère paisible et sereine.

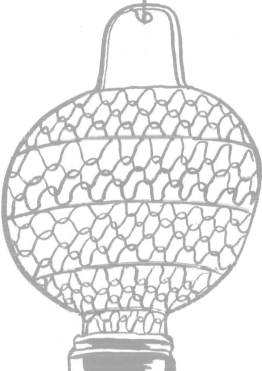

BAMBOO WALL / BADALING

LEFT PAGE:
In the living room, Kengo Kuma displays his mastery of engawa – blurring the distinction between interior and exterior spaces.

RIGHT PAGE:
The tea room, in a bamboo pavilion at the center of the house, seems to float above a water-filled moat.

LINKE SEITE:
Kengo Kuma beherrscht das engawa, die Aufhebung der Grenzen zwischen Innen- und Außenraum, meisterhaft.

RECHTE SEITE:
Der Teesalon in einem Bambus-Pavillon scheint über dem Wassergraben zu schweben.

PAGE DE GAUCHE :
Dans le séjour, Kengo Kuma montre sa maîtrise de l'engawa, la fusion entre l'intérieur et l'extérieur.

PAGE DE DROITE :
Le salon de thé, dans un pavillon en bambou au centre de la maison, semble flotter sur un bassin d'eau.

24

LEFT ABOVE:
Traditional Chinese calligraphy brushes.

LEFT BELOW:
Kuma balances "delicacy and roughness." Here, natural stone floors contrast with the airy bamboo supports.

RIGHT ABOVE:
Picture windows in the sitting room make it seem as if you can reach out and touch the grass and trees outside.

RIGHT BELOW:
One of six bedrooms in the Bamboo Wall. Each bedroom has a private bath.

LINKS OBEN:
Traditionelle chinesische Kalligrafie-Pinsel.

LINKS UNTEN:
Kuma setzt auf Kontraste: Zerbrechliches trifft auf Raues wie etwa bei diesem Boden aus Naturstein und den luftigen Bambus-stützen.

RECHTE SEITE OBEN:
Zum Greifen nah: die Gräser und Bäume, die durch die Fenster im Wohnraum zu sehen sind.

RECHTE SEITE UNTEN:
Eines der sechs Schlaf-zimmer mit Privat-Bade-zimmer im Bamboo Wall.

À GAUCHE, EN HAUT :
Des pinceaux de calligraphie traditionnelle chinoise.

À GAUCHE, EN BAS :
Kuma équilibre la « délica-tesse et la rugosité ». Ici, des dalles en pierre brute contrastent avec les colon-nes aériennes en bambou.

PAGE DE DROITE, EN HAUT :
À travers les grandes fenêtres du salon, on croirait pouvoir toucher les herbes et les arbres au dehors.

PAGE DE DROITE, EN BAS :
Une des six chambres à coucher. Chacune a sa propre salle de bains.

colour. S...

Thai sugar consumption is about the ...
languid ability to doze in the most uncomfortable positions is down ... only to
heat, work or digesting sticky rice, but also due to bloodsugar energy mounting until
the inevitable collapse.

Thais balance flavours in both food and life. Flatterers are dubbed *pak waan* (sweet
mouth) and dainty women sao waan (sweet maidens), in contrast to sassy *sao
priao* (sour maidens), and people who are stingily *khem* (salty) or sorrowfully *khom
kheun* (bitter).

In food, this balance seems a model of moderation until you realise it means that
sugar gets added to everything. Even savouries can't be sweet enough. Curries are
ladled with coconut milk, brown palm sugar's used everywhere, and even dried sliv-
ers of pork, beef or squid come saturated in syrup. Calorie counters look on aghast
... the wok-handler clacks, tings, sizzles and scrapes a healthy stir-fry then heaves in
... the table ... most lunches get laced with: lime, vinegar, chili

about as nonchalantly as my Japanese and Thai brothers.

Once happy in your birthday suit, the bath hopping begins. We counted five, from the warm soda bath infused with CO_2 to the near scalding jet bath and main onsen, both of which use the aforementioned Ranong mineral water. There's also a semi open-air garden bath that the old Japanese gents like to have a good chinwag around, a couple of steam rooms and a cold bath to sink into when you're feeling the heat.

How did we feel after an hour of or of soaking and steaming? Glowing, relaxed and super clean. If someone rubbed you with chamois leather after a session here you would squeak. But there's a spiritually cleansing dimension to bath

(i.e. cool), it's a fetching garment that you can even buy if you become attached to it.

The above are all fairly standard features at super sentōs in Japan. However, according to Smith, Yunor one thing different: combines I with Th__ _____

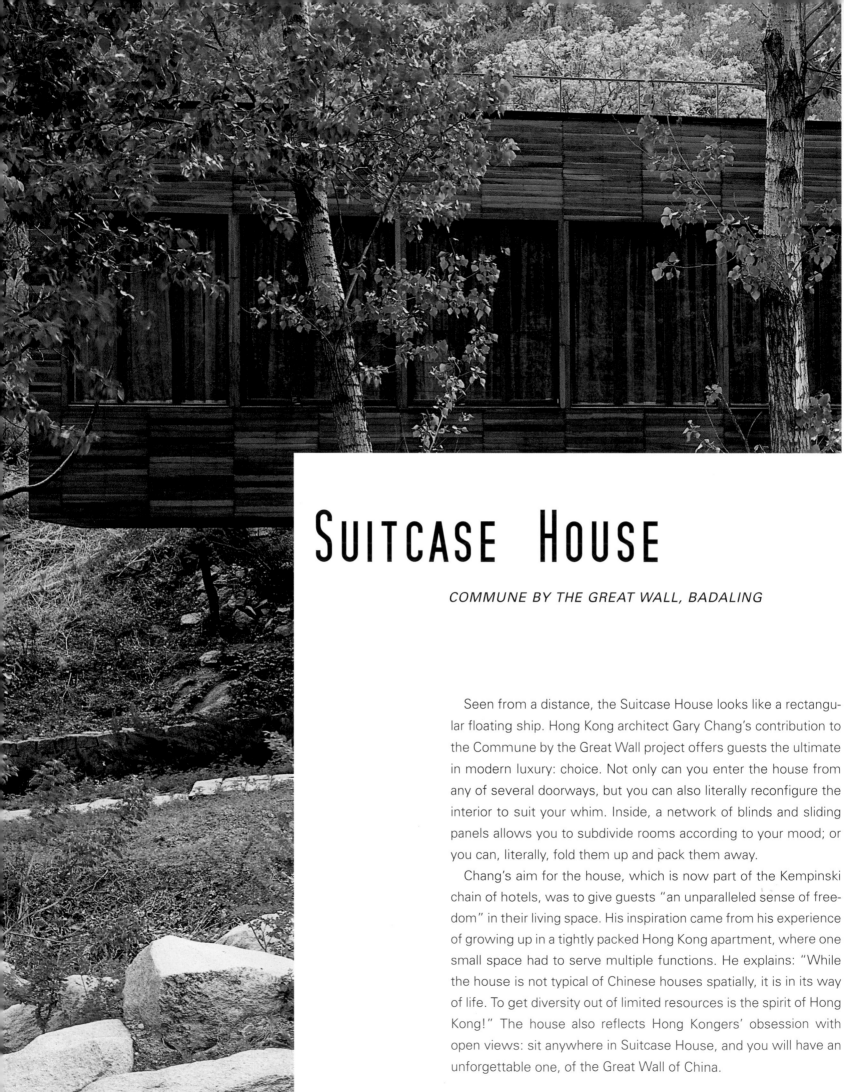

SUITCASE HOUSE

COMMUNE BY THE GREAT WALL, BADALING

Seen from a distance, the Suitcase House looks like a rectangular floating ship. Hong Kong architect Gary Chang's contribution to the Commune by the Great Wall project offers guests the ultimate in modern luxury: choice. Not only can you enter the house from any of several doorways, but you can also literally reconfigure the interior to suit your whim. Inside, a network of blinds and sliding panels allows you to subdivide rooms according to your mood; or you can, literally, fold them up and pack them away.

Chang's aim for the house, which is now part of the Kempinski chain of hotels, was to give guests "an unparalleled sense of freedom" in their living space. His inspiration came from his experience of growing up in a tightly packed Hong Kong apartment, where one small space had to serve multiple functions. He explains: "While the house is not typical of Chinese houses spatially, it is in its way of life. To get diversity out of limited resources is the spirit of Hong Kong!" The house also reflects Hong Kongers' obsession with open views: sit anywhere in Suitcase House, and you will have an unforgettable one, of the Great Wall of China.

27

Das Suitcase House sieht von Weitem aus wie ein rechteckiges Schiff, das seine Segel Richtung Große Mauer gehisst hat. Die Hotel-Villa, ein Beitrag des Hongkonger Architekten Gary Chang zur Commune by the Great Wall, bietet den Gästen das Maximum an Luxus: die Möglichkeit, den Lebensraum individuell gestalten zu können. Das lange, schmale Haus mit mehreren Eingängen kann man dank verschieb- und zusammenfaltbarer Wände aus wunderschönem Yunnan-Teakholz nach eigenen Wünschen umgestalten.

Gary Chang ließ sich für die Villa, die nun zur Kempinski-Hotelgruppe gehört, von der engen Hongkonger Wohnung inspirieren, in der er aufwuchs. Sie bestand, wie die meisten Apartments in Hongkong, aus einem einzigen kleinen Raum, der multifunktional genutzt wurde – ganz anders als bei typisch chinesischen Häusern. Zur Hongkonger Lebensart gehört deshalb, aus beschränkten Möglichkeiten das Beste zu machen, und die Begeisterung für eine freie Aussicht. Deshalb ist das Suitcase House so angelegt, dass man von jeder Seite der Villa auf die imposante Große Mauer blicken kann.

De loin, la Suitcase House évoque un navire rectangulaire voguant vers la Grande Muraille. La contribution de l'architecte de Hong-Kong Gary Chang à la Commune by the Great Wall offre le summum du luxe moderne : le choix. Il y a plusieurs portes d'entrée et on peut reconfigurer l'intérieur à sa guise. L'espace long et étroit est équipé d'un réseau équilibré de stores et de panneaux coulissants (dans un superbe teck du Yunnan) qui permet de créer et de diviser des pièces selon son humeur. Quand on n'en a plus envie, il suffit de tout replier.

L'objectif de Chang était de créer « une sensation incomparable de liberté ». Il s'est inspiré de son expérience, ayant grandi dans un de ces appartements exigus de Hong-Kong où chaque petite pièce a plusieurs usages. « Si la maison n'est pas typiquement chinoise en termes d'espace, elle l'est par son esprit. Puiser la diversité dans des ressources limitées, c'est tout Hong-Kong ! » La maison, appartenant aujourd'hui à la chaîne Kempinski, reflète une autre priorité des habitants de Hong-Kong frustrés d'espace : la vue. Où que vous soyez assis, elle est imprenable sur la Grande Muraille.

LEFT ABOVE:
The long space can also be configured in open-loft style. Floor-to-ceiling double-glazed folding doors can be opened for a porch effect.

LEFT BELOW:
In a few moments, a sequence of small rooms transforms into an open dining area with views of the Great Wall.

RIGHT ABOVE:
A guest bedroom can be hidden or revealed, as needed, by a sliding floor panel.

RIGHT BELOW:
Gary Chang designed the house for maximum flexibility. This section of the house allows guests to create small private rooms for meditation or massage.

LINKE SEITE OBEN:
Der lange, schmale Raum kann in ein offenes Loft verwandelt werden. Öffnet man die doppelt verglasten deckenhohen Schiebetüren, wird daraus eine Veranda.

LINKE SEITE UNTEN:
Einige Handgriffe – und schon verwandeln sich ein paar kleine Räume in einen einzigen, großen Essraum. Durch die Fenster sieht man auf die Große Mauer.

RECHTS OBEN:
Je nach Bedürfnis kann aus dem Gästezimmer durch die verschiebbare Wand ein offener oder geschlossener Raum gemacht werden.

RECHTS UNTEN:
Gary Changs Bau bietet maximale Flexibilität: Dieser Teil des Hauses kann als Meditations- oder Massageraum abgetrennt werden.

PAGE DE GAUCHE, EN HAUT :
Le long espace peut aussi être transformé en loft. Les hautes portes-fenêtres en double vitrage se replient en créant un effet véranda.

PAGE DE GAUCHE, EN BAS :
En quelques instants, une enfilade de petites pièces devient une grande salle à manger avec vues sur la Grande Muraille.

À DROITE, EN HAUT :
Une chambre à coucher peut être cachée ou dévoilée par un panneau coulissant.

À DROITE, EN BAS :
Gary Chang a cherché à obtenir une flexibilité maximum. Cette partie de la maison permet de créer des petits salons privés pour la méditation ou les massages.

SUITCASE HOUSE / BADALING

RED CAPITAL RANCH

HUAIROU DISTRICT

Red Capital is the title of entrepreneur-lawyer Laurence Brahm's tongue-in-cheek book about the shift of global wealth – and consumer desire – towards the East. But China-savvy travelers will recognize the phrase as the brand name of Brahm's growing collection of fabulous, quintessentially Chinese boutique resorts. Red Capital Residence, opened in 2001, transformed a classic courtyard house near the Forbidden City into a nostalgic, memorabilia-filled tribute to the era of Mao Zedong.

Sophisticated travelers visiting the Great Wall of China head for this intimate ten-villa resort, a restored Qing Dynasty hunting lodge, because it is near the Mutianyu section of the wall, far from the madding crowd. From the Ranch, there's even a private walkway leading to China's number one architectural wonder. And when you return from your private Great Wall visit, you can sit and watch the wildlife from the Ranch's open-air animal viewing platform. Inside, the villas delight the senses with brightly painted Manchurian, Mongolian, and Tibetan antiques; they also feed the soul: each room is guarded by an antique stone "animal spirit" to keep of bad vibrations.

PREVIOUS DOUBLE PAGE:
The Red Capital Ranch is a former nobleman's hunting retreat, located in a mountainous area in the Mutianyu district, near Beijing.

LEFT PAGE:
The animal viewing platform of Red Capital Ranch, surrounded by lush forest.

LEFT:
Behind a brick wall, guests enter the former wood and stone hunting lodge.

VORIGE DOPPELSEITE:
Die Red Capital Ranch, das ehemalige Jagdanwesen eines Adligen, liegt in den Bergen von Mutianyu in der Nähe von Peking.

LINKE SEITE:
Die Holzveranda der Red Capital Ranch mitten im lauschigen Wald dient als Tierbeobachtungsposten.

LINKS:
Hinter der Backsteinwand liegt der Gästeeingang des ehemaligen Jagdhauses aus Holz und Stein.

DOUBLE PAGE PRÉCÉDENTE :
Red Capital Ranch, ancien relais de chasse d'un aristocrate, est situé dans les montagnes de la région de Mutianyu, près de Pékin.

PAGE DE GAUCHE :
La terrasse d'où l'on peut observer la faune, au cœur d'une forêt luxuriante.

À GAUCHE :
Derrière le mur en brique, l'entrée de l'ancien pavillon de chasse en bois et pierre.

33

Red Capital ist der Titel des Buches von Unternehmer und Anwalt Laurence Brahm. Es ist eine ironische Beschreibung des globalen Kapitalflusses Richtung Fernost. Der China-Kenner erkennt den Namen aber auch in Brahms traumhaften, typisch chinesischen Boutique-Hotels. Zunächst eröffnete Brahm 2001 die Red Capital Residence in einem klassischen Innenhofhaus in der Nähe der Verbotenen Stadt. Daraus machte er eine nostalgische Hommage an die Ära Mao Zedongs.

2005 kam eine weitere Perle hinzu, die Red Capital Ranch, ein Luxusresort an der Großen Mauer. Dieser private, aus zehn Villen bestehende Komplex in einem restaurierten Jagdanwesen aus der Qing-Dynastie liegt fernab der Massen bei Mutianyu. Von der Ranch führt ein Privatweg direkt zur Chinesischen Mauer. Auf der hauseigenen Holzveranda kann man sich beim Beobachten von Vögeln und Wildtieren entspannen. Die Villen mit leuchtend bunten mandschurischen, mongolischen und tibetischen Antiquitäten nähren die Sinne und die Seele. Und jedes Zimmer wird von einem antiken „Tiergeist" aus Stein bewacht.

Red Capital est le titre d'un ouvrage ironique de l'avocat Laurence Brahm sur le glissement vers l'Est de la richesse mondiale et de la consommation. Mais le voyageur avisé y reconnaîtra aussi le nom de sa chaîne de superbes hôtels boutiques résolument chinois. Red Capital Residence, ouverte en 2001, est une ancienne demeure près de la Cité Interdite réaménagée en hommage nostalgique à l'ère de Mao Tsê-tung. Avec Red Capital Ranch, inauguré en 2005, Brahm a ajouté une nouvelle retraite de luxe à sa collection de joyaux.

Ce complexe de 10 villas, ancien relais de chasse de la dynastie Qing, est situé loin de la foule près du tronçon de Mutianyu de la Grande Muraille. Depuis le ranch, un chemin privé mène à la merveille architecturale. De retour de votre visite, vous pouvez admirer la faune depuis la grande terrasse d'observation. Le décor des villas ravit les sens avec un riche assortiment d'antiquités mandchoues, mongoles et tibétaines. Chaque chambre est équipée d'une ancienne stèle « esprit animal » pour vous protéger des mauvaises vibrations qui pourraient gâcher votre séjour idyllique.

LEFT ABOVE:
A double suite room with Tibetan silk pillows and a Tibetan wall carving.

LEFT BELOW:
Each room at Red Capital Ranch is appointed with modern luxury amenities. There's also a spa on the premises.

RIGHT ABOVE:
A picture-perfect view of the Mutianyu countryside, an area close to the Great Wall of China.

RIGHT BELOW:
Guests can relax and take tea on the wooden platform, decorated with Manchurian and Chinese antiques.

LINKS OBEN:
Eine Doppelzimmer-Suite mit tibetischen Seidenkissen und Wandskulptur.

LINKS UNTEN:
Jedes Zimmer der Red Capital Ranch ist mit modernen Annehmlichkeiten ausgestattet. Zur Anlage gehört auch ein Spa.

RECHTE SEITE OBEN:
Postkartenansicht von Mutianyu, einer Gegend in der Nähe der Großen Mauer Chinas.

RECHTE SEITE UNTEN:
Gäste können sich auf der Holzveranda entspannen und Tee trinken. Sie ist mit mandschurischen und chinesischen Antiquitäten möbliert.

À GAUCHE, EN HAUT :
Une double suite, avec des boiseries sculptées et des coussins en soie tibétains.

À GAUCHE, EN BAS :
Chaque chambre est équipée de tout le confort moderne. Red Capital Ranch possède également un spa.

PAGE DE DROITE, EN HAUT :
Une vue de carte postale sur la végétation de Mutianyu, une zone proche de la Grande Muraille.

PAGE DE DROITE, EN BAS :
La terrasse en bois, où l'on peut se détendre en buvant un thé, est décorée d'antiquités mandchoues et chinoises.

RED CAPITAL RANCH / HUAIROU DISTRICT

LEFT PAGE:
The renovation preserved the original stone walls and wooden beams of the historic hunting lodge, which is rich in heavy wooden Tibetan antique furniture.

RIGHT PAGE:
The snow lions painted on the chair, and the tiger skin painting above, are symbols of fearlessness.

LINKE SEITE:
Die originalen Steinwände und Holzbalken des historischen Jagdhauses mit massiven, antiken tibetischen Möbeln wurden behutsam restauriert.

RECHTE SEITE:
Die Schneelöwen-Motive auf dem Stuhl und das Bild mit dem Tigerfell an der Wand sind Symbole für Furchtlosigkeit.

PAGE DE GAUCHE :
Lors de la restauration, les murs en pierre et les poutres du pavillon de chasse ont été préservés. Les lourds meubles en bois sont des antiquités tibétaines.

36 PAGE DE DROITE :
Les lions des neiges peints sur le fauteuil et le tableau représentant une peau de tigre sont des symboles de courage.

ZHANG HAOMING

BEIJING

Millionaire businessman Zhang Haoming lives in a large, modern duplex apartment near Beijing's North Fourth Ring Road that is, literally, bursting with art. Zhang, the founder of Beijing Art Now Gallery, started buying art in 2002, and he has become one of the most important art collectors in China. His current collection now comprises nearly 700 paintings, sculptures, and photographs by contemporary Chinese artists. Local curators have nicknamed Zhang the "Chinese Saatchi." Once, he even bought an entire gallery in Sichuan province, in order to acquire just two pieces.

It's no surprise, then, that nearly every wall, table surface, and space in his family's home is a showcase of major Chinese artists, from painters Yang Shao Bin and Zhou Tiehai, to the young Sichuanese sculptor Li Zhanyang. Zhang explains that he's deliberately kept his apartment simple. There is no superfluous furniture that might interfere with his art. Even so, his collection is outstripping his square footage, so he will soon be moving with his family into a bigger house-cum-gallery. "Then I can invite my friends over every now and then to enjoy them."

Der Millionär und Geschäftsmann Zhang Haoming lebt in Peking in einer großen, modernen, mit Kunst überbordenden Maisonettewohnung in der Nähe der North Fourth Ring Road. Zhang, Gründer der Beijing Art Now Gallery, hat erst 2002 angefangen, Kunst zu sammeln, und gehört heute zu den bedeutendsten Kunstsammlern Chinas. Seine Sammlung umfasst um die 700 Gemälde, Skulpturen und Fotografien zeitgenössischer chinesischer Künstler, was Zhang den Spitznamen „chinesischer Saatchi" eingebracht hat. Einmal kaufte er eine ganze Galerie in der Provinz Sichuan, weil er nur so an die zwei Kunstwerke kam, die er unbedingt haben wollte.

An Wänden, auf Tischen und in jeder Ecke seiner Wohnung hängen oder stapeln sich Werke der wichtigsten Künstler Chinas: Yang Shao Bin, Zhou Tiehai und der junge Bildhauer Li Zhanyang aus Sichuan. Die Einrichtung der Wohnung ist bewusst zurückhaltend: nichts, was die Kunst in den Schatten stellen könnte. Die Sammlung ist nun so groß geworden, dass Zhang mit seiner Familie in ein größeres Haus – mit regulierter Temperatur und Luftfeuchtigkeit umziehen wird, damit seine Werke keinen Schaden nehmen.

Le duplex de l'homme d'affaires et millionnaire Zhang Haoming, près de North Fourth Ring Road, regorge d'œuvres d'art. Fondateur de la Beijing Art Now Gallery, il a commencé à acheter des œuvres en 2002, pour devenir l'un des plus grands collectionneurs de Chine. Surnommé par les conservateurs locaux « le Saatchi chinois », sa collection comprend près de 700 toiles, sculptures et photographies d'artistes chinois contemporains. Il a même acquis toute une galerie dans la province de Sichuan rien que pour mettre la main sur deux pièces qui lui tenaient à cœur.

Rien d'étonnant à ce que la moindre surface de son appartement soit une vitrine pour d'importants artistes, des peintres Yang Shao Bin, Zhou Tiehai et le jeune sculpteur Li Zhanyang de Sichuan. Le décor est intentionnellement sobre, sans ornements superflus ni meubles qui pourraient interférer avec l'art. L'espace ne suffisant plus à contenir sa passion, il déménagera bientôt avec sa famille dans un lieu plus grand, avec température et humidité contrôlées pour protéger les œuvres. «Ensuite, je pourrais inviter mes amis pour en profiter avec eux».

LEFT ABOVE:
The Tibetan buddhas were a gift to Zhang from a Living Buddha.

LEFT BELOW:
Whimsical erotic sculptures by Li Zhanyang frolic around the jacuzzi tub in Zhang's bathroom.

RIGHT ABOVE:
In the family living room, the portrait of a Chinese woman soldier at the left is by Qi Zhilong.

RIGHT BELOW:
Zhang's apartment is a storehouse for his huge collection of canvases and sculptures. He will soon move to a larger residence.

LINKS OBEN:
Die tibetischen Buddha-Figuren sind das Geschenk eines lebenden Buddhas.

LINKS UNTEN:
Die skurrilen, erotischen Skulpturen, Werke von Li Zhanyang, tanzen um den Jacuzzi im Badezimmer.

RECHTE SEITE OBEN:
Das Porträt einer chinesischen Soldatin im Wohnzimmer ist das Werk von Qi Zhilong.

RECHTE SEITE UNTEN:
Die Maisonettewohnung von Zhang ist auch das Lager für seine riesige Bilder- und Skulpturen-Sammlung. Bald zieht er in ein größeres Haus.

À GAUCHE, EN HAUT :
Les bouddhas tibétains ont été offerts à Zhang par un bouddha vivant.

À GAUCHE, EN BAS :
D'amusantes statuettes érotiques de Li Zhanyang batifolent autour du jacuzzi dans la salle de bains.

PAGE DE DROITE, EN HAUT :
Dans le séjour, le portrait d'une femme soldat chinoise dans le coin est de Qi Zhilong.

PAGE DE DROITE, EN BAS :
L'appartement de Zhang sert d'entrepôt à son impressionnante collection de tableaux et de sculptures. Il déménagera bientôt dans un espace plus grand.

ZHANG HAOMING, BEIJING

YANG SHAO BIN

SONGZHUANG VILLAGE, BEIJING

In 1994, Yang Shao Bin was one of the first pioneer artists to migrate from central Beijing to the countryside district of Songzhuang, a rural area dotted with farmhouses built with old blue bricks, gray tile and weather-beaten lattice windows. Since then, the artists' commune at Songzhuang has become the largest in the world, with nearly 1,000 residents. Yang, whose studio is still in Songzhuang, is now one of China's most renowned artists. His works have been seen at the Venice Biennale and are in museum collections in the U.S. and Europe.

Yang's huge open studio in a converted farmhouse with double-height ceilings allows him a neutral, quiet environment in which to create his paintings and sculptures, which often explore emotions of extreme violence and brutality (Yang's been called the "Chinese Francis Bacon"). Many of his paintings are blurry self-portraits. His latest artwork is even more personal: as part of a series about the condition of Chinese mine workers, Yang (who grew up in a Hebei mining town) is having a map of China, with locations of Chinese coal-mining accidents, tattooed on his back.

Three fiberglass sculptures in Yang Shao Bin's studio are from a series he created between 2000 and 2006.

Die drei Skulpturen aus Fiberglas in Yang Shao Bins Atelier stammen aus einer zwischen 2000 und 2006 entstandenen Serie.

Dans l'atelier de Yang Shao Bin, trois sculptures en fibre de verre appartenant à une série créée entre 2000 et 2006.

Yang Shao Bin gehörte 1994 zu den ersten Künstlern, die Peking verließen, um sich im ländlichen Songzhuang mit seinen Bauernhäusern aus blauen Backsteinen, grauen Ziegeln und verwitterten Sprossenfenstern niederzulassen. Seither ist die Gemeinschaft in Songzhuang mit fast tausend Mitgliedern zur größten Künstlerkommune der Welt angewachsen. Yang gehört mittlerweile zu den international bekanntesten und anerkanntesten Künstlern Chinas. Seine Werke wurden auf der Biennale in Venedig gezeigt, und Museen in den USA und Europa nehmen sie in ihre Sammlungen auf.

Sein riesiges Atelier befindet sich in einem umgebauten Bauernhaus mit doppelter Deckenhöhe. In dieser neutralen, ruhigen Umgebung schafft Yang Bilder und Skulpturen, die extreme Gewalt und Brutalität darstellen. Yang wird oft als „chinesischer Francis Bacon" bezeichnet. Viele seiner Bilder sind verschwommene Selbstporträts. Sein letztes Werk, eine Serie über Minenarbeiter in China, ist noch persönlicher: Yang, der in einer Minenstadt der Provinz Hebei aufwuchs, hat auf seinen Rücken eine Karte Chinas mit allen Unfallorten in Kohlebergwerken tätowieren lassen.

En 1994, Yang Shao Bin fut l'un des premiers à quitter le centre de Pékin pour Songzhuang, une campagne parsemée de fermes en briques bleues, tuiles grises et fenêtres à croisillons. Depuis, c'est devenu la plus grande communauté d'artistes au monde, comptant près de 1000 résidents. Yang, lui, est aujourd'hui un des artistes chinois les plus connus et respectés de la scène internationale, exposant à la biennale de Venise et figurant dans les collections permanentes de musées de toute l'Europe et des États-Unis.

Son immense atelier dans une ancienne ferme avec double hauteur sous plafond lui offre un environnement neutre et paisible où créer ses sculptures et ses peintures, qui explorent souvent des émotions d'une violence et d'une brutalité extrêmes. Connu pour ses autoportraits flous, on le surnomme le « Francis Bacon chinois ». Son dernier projet est encore plus personnel et traite des conditions de vie des mineurs chinois. Yang, qui a grandi dans la ville minière d'Hebei, s'est fait tatouer sur le dos une carte de la Chine indiquant toutes les mines de charbon où se sont produits des accidents.

LEFT:
Works in progress at Yang's studio. On the table, left, a traditional Chinese set of Yixing teapots and cups stands ready to welcome visitors.

RIGHT ABOVE:
A new painting, one of Yang's series of emotional self-portraits, in maroon and pink.

RIGHT BELOW:
Another view of Yang's fiberglass sculptures. The studio is filled with natural light that comes in from overhead skylights.

LINKE SEITE:
Unvollendete Werke im Atelier. Die Teekannen und -tassen auf dem Tisch sind aus Yixing-Keramik und stehen für Gäste bereit.

RECHTS OBEN:
Das Gemälde in Braun und Rot gehört zu Yangs Serie expressiver Selbstporträts.

RECHTS UNTEN:
Durch die Oberlichter des Ateliers scheint das Sonnenlicht auf Yangs Fiberglas-Skulpturen.

PAGE DE GAUCHE :
Des œuvres en cours dans l'atelier. Sur la table, un service à thé traditionnel de Yixing attend les visiteurs.

À DROITE, EN HAUT :
Une nouvelle peinture, un des autoportraits émotionnels de Yang, en bordeaux et rose.

À DROITE, EN BAS :
Une autre vue des sculptures en fibre de verre. Les verrières du toit inondent l'atelier de lumière naturelle.

YANG SHAO BIN / SONGZHUANG VILLAGE, BEIJING

WANG MAI

798 DASHANZI ART DISTRICT, BEIJING

The 798 Dashanzi Art District is practically synonymous with the contemporary Chinese art scene. Over the last six years, the crème of China's artists have settled into these abandoned factory buildings built in 1957 by East German engineers in the Bauhaus style. Today the district is a hub of artistic activity, famous for its galleries, bookshops, studio spaces, clubs and cafes. Wang Mai's studio, in the eastern part of the district, occupies a building that used to be a munitions factory; he's transformed the industrial space into a comfortable home for his creative energies.

Wang is a multi-media artist whose work explores the relationships between old and new China, tradition and capitalism. The eight rooms of his studio give him enough room to stretch out and work on paintings, sculpture, drawings, photography and installations at the same time. (And, when he needs a break, there's a table tennis set, too). Wang's 798 space is not only a backdrop for his work; it has also been an inspiration. He's used hundreds of wooden molds found in the factory to make imposing sculptures that seem to watch over him as he works, like robot Buddhas.

LEFT PAGE:
The image of Mao Zedong is an untitled painting by Wang Mai.

LEFT:
Artist Wang Mai prefers working in the daytime, in the inner room of his studio in Beijing's 798 Dashanzi Art District.

LINKE SEITE:
Wang Mais Porträt von Mao Zedong ist ohne Titel.

LINKS:
Tagsüber arbeitet Wang Mai im innersten Raum seines Ateliers im 798 Dashanzi Art District in Peking.

PAGE DE GAUCHE :
Un tableau sans titre de Wang Mai représentant Mao Tsê-Tung.

À GAUCHE :
Wang Mai aime travailler à la lumière du jour dans une pièce aveugle de son atelier du district de 798 Dashanzi Art à Pékin.

Der 798 Dashanzi Art District ist zum Synonym für die zeitgenössische Kunstszene Chinas geworden. Die 1957 von ostdeutschen Ingenieuren im Bauhausstil errichteten Fabrikgebäude wurden in den letzten Jahren von der chinesischen Künstlerelite entdeckt. Heute ist 798 mit seinen Galerien, Buchläden, Ateliers, Clubs und Cafés zu einem kreativen Zentrum Chinas geworden. Das Atelier von Wang Mai befindet sich in einer ehemaligen Munitionsfabrik im östlichen Teil des Geländes. Aus dem einst industriell genutzten Raum machte er eine komfortable Wohnstätte.

Wang, ein Multi-Media-Künstler, findet seine Inspiration in Spannungsfeld zwischen dem alten und neuen China, der Tradition und dem Kapitalismus. Sein Atelier verfügt über acht Räume. Er hat damit genug Platz, gleichzeitig an seinen Gemälden, Skulpturen, Zeichnungen, Fotografien und Installationen zu arbeiten, und für eine Tischtennisplatte, an der er sich zwischendurch eine kleine Pause gönnt. Wang hat, als er in die ehemalige Fabrik einzog, Hunderte Holzformen gefunden und sie für seine eindrucksvollen Skulpturen wiederverwendet.

Le district 798 de Dashanzi Art est pratiquement synonyme du monde de l'art contemporain chinois. Au cours des six dernières années, la crème des artistes a envahi ses usines désaffectées construites en 1957 par des ingénieurs est-allemands dans le style Bauhaus. Aujourd'hui, le quartier est connu pour ses galeries, librairies, ateliers, clubs et cafés. Wang Mai s'est installé dans une ancienne fabrique de munitions dans l'est du district. Il a transformé l'espace industriel en une demeure confortable où donner le champ libre à sa créativité.

Wang est un artiste multimédia qui explore les relations entre la Chine d'hier et d'aujourd'hui, la tradition et le capitalisme. Ses huit pièces lui permettent de travailler en même temps sur ses peintures, ses sculptures, ses dessins, sa photographie et ses installations (et de jouer au ping-pong de temps en temps). Son atelier est également une source d'inspiration : il y a trouvé des centaines de moules en bois avec lesquels il a réalisé d'imposantes sculptures qui semblent veiller sur son travail tels des bouddhas robots.

Hundreds of old wooden manufacturing molds, made by Chinese workers in the 1950s and 1960s, were left behind in Wang's abandoned factory space; he recycles them for his sculptures like the one in this picture, "The Fertility of Capitalism".

In der ehemaligen Munitionsfabrik entdeckte Wang Hunderte alter Holzformen. Sie wurden in den 1950ern und 1960ern von chinesischen Arbeitern hergestellt. Nun verwendet er sie für seine Skulpturen wie die im Bild zu sehende „Fruchtbarkeit des Kapitalismus".

Dans l'usine désaffectée, Wang a trouvé des centaines de moules en bois réalisés par des ouvriers chinois dans les années 1950 et 1960. Il les a recyclés en sculptures telles que celle-ci, intitulée « La Fertilité du capitalisme ».

50

WANG MAI / 798 DASHANZI ART DISTRICT, BEIJING

LEFT ABOVE:
Wang Mai with his sculpture installation, "Diverse".

LEFT BELOW:
A small kitchen area is hidden behind an opaque screen made of steel and plastic.

RIGHT:
Wang Mai's studio has a small entertaining area where he greets guests. He also has a ping-pong table.

LINKS OBEN:
Wang Mai mit seiner Skulpturen-Installation „Diverse".

LINKS UNTEN:
Hinter der opaken Trennwand aus Stahl und Plastik liegt eine kleine Küche.

RECHTE SEITE:
Kleiner Aufenthaltsraum für Gäste im Atelier. Hier steht auch eine Tischtennisplatte.

À GAUCHE, EN HAUT :
Wang avec son installation de sculptures, « Diverse ».

À GAUCHE, EN BAS :
Une petite cuisine cachée derrière une cloison opaque en acier et plastique.

PAGE DE DROITE :
L'atelier comporte un petit salon pour recevoir ainsi qu'une table de ping-pong.

Shao Fan & Anna Liu Li

SHUNYI DISTRICT, BEIJING

The artist Shao Fan, known for his radical deconstructions of traditional Chinese furniture, had always dreamed of building his own house. A few years ago, he bought a large tract of land in a suburban Beijing neighborhood. Dividing the property among himself and five friends, Shao Fan designed a complex that challenges the norms of Western-style housing, and updates the traditional Chinese approach to living space. Shao Fan calls his building style "contemporary courtyard living" – in effect, he's modernized the *hutong* and moved it to the suburbs.

Shao Fan's own house is the prize of the complex, which is surrounded by a high wall made of blue bricks. As in the traditional Beijing courtyard house, or *si he yuan*, the living area consists of a series of rooms arranged around two main courtyards – one containing rare plum trees, a popular subject in Chinese poetry and painting. Inside, Shao Fan's own chair-sculptures seem to float in mid-air, alongside perfect, ancient Buddha statues and an 8,000 year old piece of jade. The décor is spare, but this house feels full, for it holds within its blue walls all the promise of contemporary China.

55

Der Künstler Shao Fan, bekannt für beeindruckende Dekonstruktionen traditioneller chinesischer Möbel, träumte schon immer davon, sein eigenes Haus zu bauen. Vor ein paar Jahren erwarb er ein großes Grundstück in einem Pekinger Vorort und teilte es zwischen sich und fünf Freunden auf. Der Gebäudekomplex, den er dafür entworfen hat, stellt die Prinzipien der westlichen Bauart auf den Kopf und modernisiert gleichzeitig die traditionelle Lebensweise des *hutong*, den er in die Vorstadt gebracht hat.

Shao Fans Haus, umgeben von hohen Mauern aus blauen Backsteinen, ist das herausragendste auf dem Grundstück. Wie in einem traditionellen Pekinger Innenhofhaus, einem *si he yuan*, sind die Wohnräume um zwei große Innenhöfe angelegt. In einem der beiden stehen seltene japanische Pflaumenbäume, in China ein beliebtes Motiv in der Dichtkunst und Malerei. Im Innern des Hauses „schweben" Shao Fans Stuhl-Skulpturen neben alten Buddha-Statuen und einem 8000 Jahre alten Stück Jade. Die Einrichtung ist spärlich, aber erfüllt alle Verheißungen, die das neue China verspricht.

L'artiste Shao Fan, connu pour ses déconstructions radicales de mobilier traditionnel chinois, avait toujours rêvé de construire sa maison de bout en bout. Après avoir acquis un grand terrain dans une banlieue de Pékin, décrite par sa femme Anna comme « pleine d'étrangers », il l'a divisé avec cinq autres amis. Puis il a bâti un complexe qui défie les normes occidentales du développement immobilier privé tout en rénovant le concept chinois de l'espace de vie. S'il a baptisé son style « vie moderne en cour », c'est qu'il s'agit d'une modernisation du *hutong*.

Sa propre demeure est le joyau du complexe ceint d'un haut mur en briques bleues. Comme dans la maison pékinoise traditionnelle, ou *si he yuan*, les pièces sont disposées autour de deux cours, dont l'une accueille des *prunus mume*, un motif apprécié dans la peinture et la poésie chinoise. À l'intérieur, ses sculptures chaises semblent flotter aux côtés de bouddhas anciens et d'un morceau de jade vieux de 8000 ans. En dépit de son décor dépouillé, la maison respire la plénitude, chargée de toutes les promesses de la Chine contemporaine.

PREVIOUS DOUBLE PAGE:
The artist, Shao Fan, at his drafting table, which he designed using traditional Chinese joinery methods instead of nails. The top is made from a single piece of wood from India, called ti li in Chinese.

RIGHT:
One of the house's several living areas. The Chinese and Tibetan furniture is arranged so that guests can appreciate the view of the rare mei hua trees that Shao Fan brought to the garden from southern China. The trees symbolize poetry and scholarship. The painting "Cloud" is by Shao Fan.

VORIGE DOPPELSEITE:
Shao Fan an seinem Zeichentisch, den er selbst entworfen hat. Nach alter chinesischer Tischler-tradition wurde kein ein-ziger Nagel verwendet. Die Platte ist aus einem Stück Holz, das aus Indien stammt und auf Chinesisch ti li heißt.

58

RECHTS:
Einer der vielen Wohn-räume. Die chinesischen und tibetischen Möbel sind so angeordnet, dass die Gäste freien Blick auf die seltenen mei hua-Bäume haben. Shao Fan hat die Bäume, die Dichtkunst und Gelehrsamkeit symbo-lisieren, in Südchina ge-kauft. Das Gemälde von Shao Fan heißt „Wolke".

DOUBLE PAGE PRÉCÉDENTE :
L'artiste Shao Fan devant sa table de dessin qu'il a conçue avec des méthodes de menuiserie traditionnelle chinoise sans le moindre clou. Le plateau est consti-tué d'un seul bloc de bois indien, appelé ti li en chinois.

À DROITE :
Un des séjours de la maison. Les fauteuils sont disposés de sorte que les invités aient vue sur les précieux mei hua que Shao Fan a rapportés du sud de la Chine pour orner la cour. Ces arbres symbolisent la poésie et l'érudition. Le tableau « Nuage » est du maître de maison.

LEFT ABOVE:
A living area. The acrylic-top table is a Shao Fan design. Anna Liu Li found the antique Chinese Buddhas in a Hong Kong shop.

LEFT BELOW:
In another living area, Shao Fan designed this wood table with two levels, to produce a "floating" effect.

RIGHT ABOVE:
Shao Fan's "Wang", a deconstructed Ming Dynasty chair. The "Wang" name refers to the Chinese character for "Emperor".

RIGHT BELOW:
Qing Dynasty Buddhas from Jiangxi province, found by Anna Liu Li. The couple met while shopping for antiques.

LINKE SEITE OBEN:
Der Acryl-Tisch ist ein Entwurf von Shao Fan. Die antiken chinesischen Buddhas hat seine Frau Anna Liu Li in einem Geschäft in Hongkong aufgestöbert.

LINKE SEITE UNTEN:
Dieser „schwebende" Holztisch mit zwei Ebenen wurde ebenfalls von Shao Fan entworfen.

RECHTS OBEN:
Shao Fans „Wang" wurde aus einem zerlegten Stuhl aus der Ming-Dynastie gestaltet. Der Name „Wang" bezieht sich auf das chinesische Symbol für Kaiser.

RECHTS UNTEN:
Die Buddhas aus der Qing-Dynastie, die Anna Liu Li entdeckt hat, stammen aus der Provinz Jiangxi. Das Paar lernte sich beim Einkauf von Antiquitäten kennen.

PAGE DE GAUCHE, EN HAUT :
Un des séjours. Le plateau de table en acrylique a été conçu par Shao Fan. Anna Liu Li a découvert les bouddhas antiques chinois dans une boutique de Hong-Kong.

PAGE DE GAUCHE, EN BAS .
Shao Fan a dessiné cette table en bois avec deux niveaux pour créer un effet de « flottement ».

À DROITE, EN HAUT :
Une chaise de la dynastie Ming « déconstruite » par Shao Fan et baptisée « Wang », d'après le caractère chinois signifiant « empereur ».

À DROITE, EN BAS :
Des bouddhas de la dynastie Qing provenant de la province de Jiangxi et trouvés par Anna Liu Li. Le couple s'est rencontré en chinant.

A reception area, with two
Shao Fan polished steel
"Ming" chairs. The painting
is also by Shao Fan.

Empfangsraum mit zwei
„Ming"-Edelstahlstühlen,
entworfen von Shao Fan.
Auch das Gemälde stammt
vom Künstler.

Dans une aire de réception,
deux chaises « Ming » en
acier poli de Shao Fan.
Le tableau est également
de lui.

62

LEFT AND RIGHT PAGE:
A guest bedroom featuring a 200-year-old Qing Dynasty mahogany bed.

LINKE UND RECHTE SEITE:
Ein Gästezimmer mit einem 200 Jahre alten Mahagoni-Bett aus der Qing-Dynastie.

PAGES DE GAUCHE ET DE DROITE :
Dans une chambre d'amis, un lit en acajou de la dynastie Qing, vieux de 200 ans.

64

SHAO FAN & ANNA LIU LI / SHUNYI DISTRICT, BEIJING

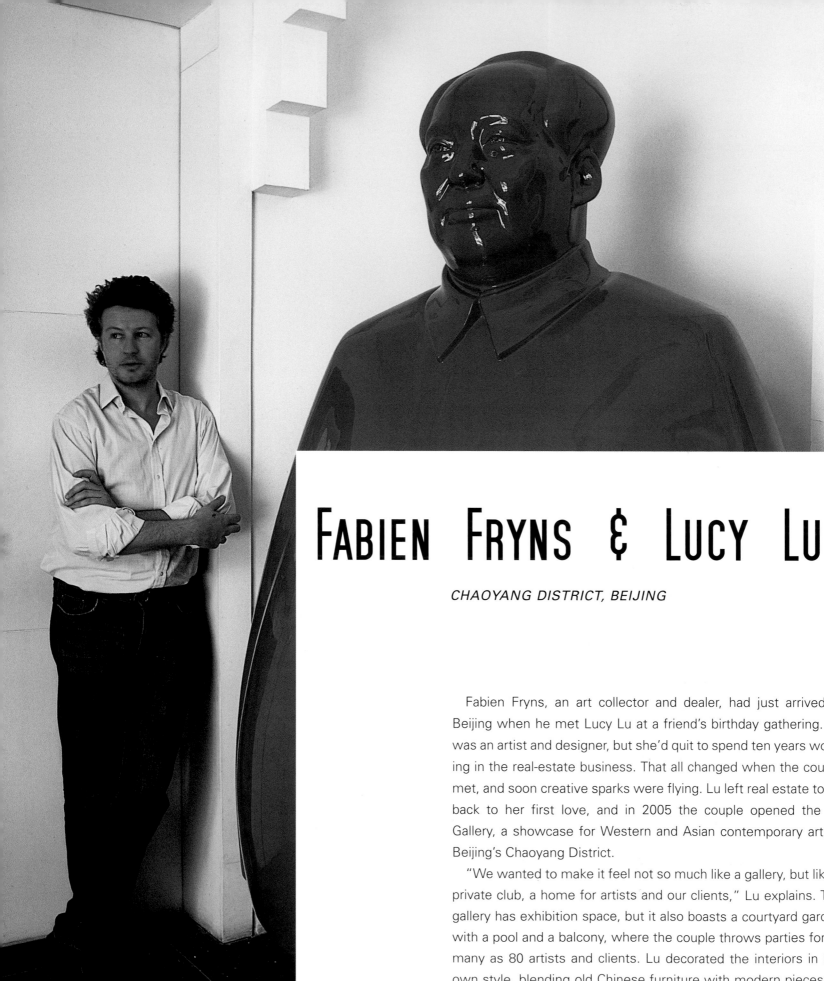

FABIEN FRYNS & LUCY LU

CHAOYANG DISTRICT, BEIJING

Fabien Fryns, an art collector and dealer, had just arrived in Beijing when he met Lucy Lu at a friend's birthday gathering. Lu was an artist and designer, but she'd quit to spend ten years working in the real-estate business. That all changed when the couple met, and soon creative sparks were flying. Lu left real estate to go back to her first love, and in 2005 the couple opened the F2 Gallery, a showcase for Western and Asian contemporary art, in Beijing's Chaoyang District.

"We wanted to make it feel not so much like a gallery, but like a private club, a home for artists and our clients," Lu explains. The gallery has exhibition space, but it also boasts a courtyard garden with a pool and a balcony, where the couple throws parties for as many as 80 artists and clients. Lu decorated the interiors in her own style, blending old Chinese furniture with modern pieces: "I like simple shapes." Attached to a private dining room is a modern kitchen where a chef from the Sichuan Province prepares lunch every day. Distinguished contemporary artists from the West and from China drop in to visit and exchange ideas and inspiration.

LEFT PAGE:
Fabien Fryns at the entrance to F2 Gallery.

LEFT:
Another corner of F2 Gallery. The purple Mao sculpture is by Zheng Lu.

LINKE SEITE:
Fabien Fryns im Eingangs-bereich der Galerie F2.

LINKS:
Leuchtend violette Mao-Skulptur von Zheng Lu.

PAGE DE GAUCHE :
Fabien Fryns dans l'entrée de la galerie F2.

À GAUCHE :
Un autre angle de la galerie F2. La statue violette de Mao est de Zheng Lu.

Fabien Fryns, ein Kunstsammler und -händler, lernte Lucy Lu kurz nach seiner Ankunft in Peking bei einer Geburtstagsfeier kennen. Lu arbeitete damals seit zehn Jahren im Immobiliengeschäft, war aber ursprünglich Künstlerin und Designerin. Beim Zusammentreffen mit Fryns sprang der kreative Funke sofort über. Lu verließ die Immobilienbranche, und das Paar eröffnete 2005 im Pekinger Viertel Chaoyang die Galerie F2 für zeitgenössische Kunst.

„Wir wollten keine gewöhnliche Galerie, sondern eher einen Privatklub, in dem sich Künstler und Kunden wie zu Hause fühlen können", erklärt Lu. So gibt es neben einem Ausstellungsraum auch noch einen Innenhofgarten mit Swimmingpool und Balkon, in dem Partys für bis zu 80 Künstler und Sammler stattfinden, und eine Wohnküche. Täglich bereitet ein Koch aus der Provinz Sichuan ein Mittagessen zu, um all die bekannten Namen der internationalen zeitgenössischen Künstlerszene zu verköstigen, die sich regelmäßig um den Tisch versammeln. Die klar strukturierte Inneneinrichtung, ein Mix aus alten chinesischen Möbeln und modernen Stücken, ist ein Entwurf Lus.

Collectionneur et marchand d'art, Fabien Fryns venait d'arriver à Pékin quand il a rencontré Lucy Lu lors d'une fête d'anniversaire. Artiste et designer, Lu avait interrompu sa carrière depuis dix ans pour se consacrer à l'immobilier. Ce coup de foudre ne pouvait que faire voler des étincelles de créativité. Lu a renoué avec ses anciennes amours et, en 2005, le couple a ouvert la galerie F2, une vitrine de l'art contemporain asiatique et occidental, dans le quartier Chaoyang de Pékin.

« Nous avons conçu la galerie comme un club privé, une maison pour nos artistes et nos clients », explique Lu. Outre l'espace d'exposition, il y a un jardin avec une piscine et un balcon où le couple donne des fêtes pour 80 personnes. Lu a décoré l'intérieur dans son style, mêlant les meubles anciens chinois et des pièces modernes: « J'aime les formes simples. » Dans la cuisine moderne, un chef venu de Sichuan prépare les déjeuners. D'éminents artistes contemporains, chinois et occidentaux passent régulièrement pour échanger des idées et chercher l'inspiration.

In the gallery's dining room, clients and artists come together for delicious Sichuan food. The artwork is by photographer and performance artist Zhang Huan.

Künstler und Sammler treffen sich in der Wohnküche der Galerie zu köstlichen Sichuan-Spezialitäten. Die Kunstwerke stammen vom Performance-Künstler und Fotografen Zhang Huan.

Dans la salle à manger de la galerie, clients et artistes se réunissent autour de délicieux plats du Sichuan. Le grand portrait est une œuvre du photographe et performer Zhang Huan.

68

FABIEN FRYNS & LUCY LU / CHAOYANG DISTRICT, BEIJING

THE CHINA CLUB

BEIJING

Every morning, in Beijing's China Club, workers in white mandarin blouses scurry about, polishing to perfection every brass plate, door lintel, and knocker in the sprawling, four-courtyard complex. It is the sort of attention to detail you would expect at a property renovated by Hong Kong's famous art collector and raconteur David Tang, founder of the Shanghai Tang fashion and home design chain. Tang's renovation of this 17th-century prince's palace near Tiananmen Square is exquisite. A stroll through the four enclosed garden spaces that connect the old Sichuan restaurant – once the favorite of Chinese leader Deng Xiaoping – with a newer bar and guesthouse building returns you to Chinese historical novels.

There are small, intimate dining rooms and meeting areas, furnished with Ming Dynasty chairs and appointed with the bright green and purple table linens and celadon pottery familiar to fans of Shanghai Tang's China-chic retro design. Best of all are the guest rooms, located on the second floor and decorated in the Shanghai style of around 1920. The view from the balcony is fit for any modern prince.

LEFT PAGE:
In the restored palace, open gates and doorways allow a glimpse of life in the courtyard.

RIGHT:
A guard in vintage Chinese military uniform welcomes guests to the China Club.

LINKE SEITE:
Durch die offenen Türen und Tore des renovierten Palastes sieht man auf das Treiben im Innenhof.

RECHTS:
Ein Wachmann in alter chinesischer Militäruniform heißt die Gäste des China Clubs willkommen.

PAGE DE GAUCHE :
Dans le palais restauré, les portes ouvertes laissent entrevoir la cour animée.

À DROITE :
Un garde en uniforme « vintage » » accueille les clients du China Club.

Allmorgendlich polieren im Pekinger China Club Angestellte in weißen China-Blusen jede Messingtafel, jede Türschwelle und jeden Türklopfer. Diese Liebe zum Detail ist typisch für den Besitzer David Tang, den Hongkonger Kunstsammler und Gründer des Designlabels Shanghai Tang, der den Prinzenpalast aus dem 17. Jahrhundert in der Nähe des Tiananmen-Platz renovierte. Das Resultat ist exquisit. Beim Spaziergang durch die vier abgeschlossenen Innenhöfe – sie verbinden das im Originalzustand belassene Restaurant Sichuan (einst Lieblingsrestaurant des Politikers Deng Xiaoping) mit der neuen Bar und dem Gästehaus – wähnt man sich auf einer Reise durch die Welt alter chinesischer Romane.

Die Stühle der behaglichen Ess- und Besprechungszimmer stammen aus der Ming-Dynastie; die sattgrünen oder violetten Tischtücher und die grüne Retro-Keramik tragen das Label von Shanghai Tang. Am schönsten sind die Gästezimmer in der zweiten Etage im opulent-sinnlichen Schanghai-Stil der 1920er, auch der Ausblick vom Balkon auf den begrünten Innenhof ist bezaubernd.

Tous les matins, dans le China Club de Pékin, des ouvrières en blouses blanches de mandarin lustrent les moindres plaques de cuivre, linteaux et heurtoirs du vaste complexe à quatre cours. C'est le soin du détail auquel on peut s'attendre chez le célèbre collectionneur d'art et conteur de Hong-Kong, David Tang, fondateur de la chaîne de boutiques de mode et de décoration Shanghai Tang. Sa restauration d'un palais princier du XVIIe siècle près de la place Tiananmen est exquise. En se promenant dans les quatre jardins clos qui relient le vieux restaurant de Sichuan, dont Deng Xiaoping était l'un des piliers, au bar et à la guesthouse plus récents, on croirait feuilleter un roman classique chinois.

Les petites salles à manger et salons intimes sont décorés de mobilier de la dynastie Ming, de linge de table vert et pourpre et de céladons bien connus des amateurs du rétro chic de Shanghai Tang. Mais le plus beau, ce sont les chambres du premier étage, luxueuses et sensuelles, très « Shanghai années 1920 ». Le balcon donne sur la cour jardin, digne d'un prince des temps modernes.

LEFT ABOVE:
Cherry trees in bloom add springtime beauty to the spacious inner courtyard.

LEFT BELOW:
A pair of overstuffed chairs in red silk brocade lends a retro Shanghai-style glamour to a guest suite.

RIGHT ABOVE:
Another view of the guest suite which features a traditional curtained Chinese platform bed and a bright red silk lamp.

RIGHT BELOW:
An antique standing lamp outside one of the six private dining rooms.

LINKE SEITE OBEN:
Frühlingshaft schön: die blühenden Kirschbäume im großen mittleren Innenhof.

LINKE SEITE UNTEN:
Glanzvolle Gästesuite: die üppigen, mit rotem Seidenbrokat gepolsterten Sessel im Retro-Schanghai-Stil.

RECHTS OBEN:
Traditionelle chinesische Bettstatt in der Gästesuite mit Vorhängen und leuchtend roter Seidenlampe.

RECHTS UNTEN:
Antike Stehlampe vor einem der sechs privaten Esszimmer.

PAGE DE GAUCHE, EN HAUT :
Au printemps, les cerisiers en fleurs embellissent encore la spacieuse cour intérieure.

PAGE DE GAUCHE, EN BAS :
Dans une des suites, de profonds fauteuils en brocart de soie rouge ajoutent une touche de glamour au décor rétro Shanghai.

À DROITE, EN HAUT :
Une autre vue de la suite avec un lit surélevé traditionnel chinois et une lampe en soie rouge vif.

À DROITE, EN BAS :
Un lampadaire ancien devant une des six salles à manger privées.

THE CHINA CLUB / BEIJING

The old Chinese platform beds were built high to accommodate a heating system underneath; an antique wooden stepstool provides access to this cozy, private enclave.

Früher wurden Betten in China erhöht auf eine Plattform gebaut, um darunter eine Heizung zu installieren. Der antike Holzschemel hilft, ins Bett zu steigen.

Les lits à plateforme chinois étaient surélevés pour accueillir un système de chauffage en dessous. On accède à cette alcôve intime et douillette par un marchepied ancien en bois.

74

A dramatic entrance: blazing Chinese lanterns welcome guests to the 17th-century palace.

Theatralisch: Dio Gäste werden mit leuchtend orangenfarbenen chinesischen Laternen im ehemaligen Palast aus dem 17. Jahrhundert begrüßt.

Une entrée théâtrale : de flamboyantes lanternes chinoises accueillent les clients dans cet ancien palais du XVIIᵉ siècle.

76

Côté Cour

DONG CHENG DISTRICT, BEIJING

Shauna Liu had always dreamed of having her own small hotel, even as she built a career as an investment banker in California and Hong Kong. But it wasn't until she traveled to Morocco that she realized she could make her dream come true in her hometown, Beijing. "I saw all those cute hotels on the narrow little streets that are so much like our Beijing *hutongs*. That's when I knew I could create my own hotel." Liu found her dream house in 2005, in a *hutong* neighborhood rich with cultural history: famous Chinese opera singers of the Imperial Court had lived here since the Ming Dynasty. She closed the deal in ten days, then spent a year renovating.

Liu kept the bones of the historic house, while transforming the interior with an artistic sensibility honed during her experiences living at home and abroad. "I lightened things up. Traditional Chinese furniture is too dark. I like to stay in an old house, but I want my bathrooms to be modern." In the Côté Cour's 14 rooms, guests enjoy a unique mixture of modern and old-fashioned Beijing lifestyles – a window in one of the courtyard walls provides a glimpse into the house of a 70-year-old neighbor.

Shauna Liu träumte schon immer von einem eigenen kleinen Hotel, auch als sie Karriere als Investment-Bankerin in Kalifornien und Hongkong machte. Eine Reise nach Marokko inspirierte sie zu einem Boutique-Hotel in ihrer Heimatstadt Peking: „Ich sah diese hübschen Hotels in den engen Straßen, die mich an die *hutongs* in Peking erinnerten." Liu fand 2005 ihr Traumhaus in einem *hutong*-Viertel, in dem seit der Ming-Dynastie kaiserliche Opernsänger lebten. Den Kaufvertrag unterzeichnete Liu sofort und verbrachte das folgende Jahr mit der Restaurierung des Gebäudes: „1600 Lastwagenladungen Schutt wurden abtransportiert, und manchmal waren 30 Handwerker gleichzeitig an der Arbeit."

An der Struktur des historischen Hauses änderte Liu nichts. Das Innere verwandelte sie mit viel Fingerspitzengefühl. Heute ist das Hotel mit 14 Zimmern eine einzigartige Melange aus modernem und traditionellem Pekinger Stil. „Ich liebe alte Häuser, aber auch moderne Badezimmer", sagt Liu. Durch ein Fenster in einer der Mauern des Innenhofs sieht man auf das Haus einer 70-jährigen Nachbarin. Liu: „Den Gästen sage ich, sie gehöre zum Dekor."

Tout en poursuivant sa carrière de banquière en Californie et à Hong Kong, Shauna Liu rêvait d'avoir son propre hôtel boutique jusqu'à ce qu'un voyage au Maroc achève de la convaincre. « Quand j'ai vu ces charmants petits hôtels dans des ruelles qui ressemblaient tant à nos *hutongs*, je me suis enfin décidée. » En 2005, elle a trouvé le lieu de ses rêves dans un quartier historique de son Pékin natal. Les chanteurs d'opéra de la cour impériale y vivaient et y répétaient depuis la dynastie Ming. L'affaire fut bouclée en dix jours, suivis d'un an de travaux. « Nous avons évacué 1600 camions de gravats. Certains jours, 30 artisans travaillaient dans la cour en même temps ».

Liu a conservé l'ossature et transformé l'intérieur avec un sens artistique affiné par ses séjours en Chine et à l'étranger, créant 14 chambres dans un style mêlant l'ancien et le moderne. « J'ai éclairci les meubles traditionnels, trop sombres. J'aime les vieilles maisons mais je voulais des salles de bains modernes. » Dans une cour, une ouverture donne sur la maison de la voisine de 70 ans. « Elle fait partie du décor. »

LEFT ABOVE:
In her renovation, Liu restored traditional details like the tile roof and wooden columns.

LEFT BELOW:
The relaxing lounge area, featuring at right with an ornamental bird cage.

RIGHT ABOVE:
The Buddha statue is from Thailand; the contemporary Chinese painting is by Liu's friend, artist Chi Peng.

RIGHT BELOW:
Liu designed the table and chairs, which bear the hotel's red logo.

LINKE SEITE OBEN:
Traditionelle Elemente wie das Ziegeldach und die Holzsäulen restaurierte Liu mit großer Sorgfalt.

LINKE SEITE UNTEN:
Behagliche Lounge mit dekorativem Vogelkäfig in der rechten Ecke des Raums.

RECHTS OBEN:
Die Buddha-Statue stammt aus Thailand; das Bild ist ein Werk von Chi Peng, der mit Liu befreundet ist.

RECHTS UNTEN:
Entwürfe von Liu: runder Tisch und Stühle mit dem roten Logo des Hotels.

PAGE DE GAUCHE, EN HAUT :
Liu a restauré des détails traditionnels tels que les tuiles du toit et les colonnes en bois.

PAGE DE GAUCHE, EN BAS :
Le coin salon, avec une cage ornementale à droite.

À DROITE, EN HAUT :
Le bouddha vient de Thaïlande. Le tableau est de Chi Peng, un ami de Liu.

À DROITE, EN BAS :
Liu a dessiné les tables et les chaises qui portent le logo rouge de l'hôtel.

CÔTÉ COUR / DONG CHENG DISTRICT, BEIJING

KELLY LI HONG YU

CHAOYANG DISTRICT, BEIJING

Interior designer Kelly Li Hong Yu's home is a sanctuary of calm, stability, and culture. Four years ago, Li, who has lived in Beijing for 20 years, found a four-room duplex apartment in a modern high-rise building, that featured an abundance of one thing that can be hard to find in China's capital: "The space is filled with sun at all times of the day." Together with her ex-husband, Simon, and designer friend Muo Ping, Li created a clean and contemporary look. Furnishings are kept simple. The transparent stairs that lead from the living room to the upstairs bedrooms seem to float in midair. And there's absolutely no clutter; only a few carefully chosen paintings and objects that reflect Li's love of Chinese and Asian culture.

There's a story behind every object, but the best one is the tale of the intricately carved eight-foot Qing Dynasty wooden folding screen. It is from the house of Li Lian Ying, the infamous last eunuch in the Chinese Imperial Court, who was the favorite of the Dowager Empress Cixi. This treasure of Chinese history has been the backdrop for intrigues, plots, and conspiracies; now it has a new life in Li's serene, modern Beijing apartment.

Die Wohnung der Interior-Designerin Kelly Li Hong Yu ist eine Oase mitten im Getümmel Pekings. Li, die seit 20 Jahren in Peking lebt, fand diese Vierzimmer-Maisonettewohnung vor vier Jahren in einem modernen Hochhaus. Sie ist zu jeder Tageszeit lichtdurchflutet – ein seltener Luxus in Peking. Zusammen mit ihrem Ex-Mann Simon und dem befreundeten Designer Muo Ping kreierte Li einen schnörkellos-zeitgemäßen Look passend zu den Lichtverhältnissen und zum Panorama des Chaoyang-Viertels.

Eine transparente Treppe – sie scheint mitten im Raum zu schweben – führt vom Wohnzimmer in die oben gelegenen Schlafzimmer. Nur ein paar ausgesuchte Bilder und Objekte zeugen von Lis Liebe zur chinesischen und asiatischen Kultur. Jedes dieser Objekte hat eine Geschichte: Lis Prachtstück, der faltbare, kunstvoll geschnitzte, zweieinhalb Meter hohe Holzparavent aus der Qing-Dynastie gehörte einst Li Lian Ying, einem der letzten Eunuchen am kaiserlichen Hof und Günstling der „Kaiserinwitwe" Cixi. Dieses wertvolle Geschenk eines Freundes hat höfische Intrigen, Verschwörungen und Eifersuchtsdramen miterlebt.

La maison de la décoratrice Kelly Li Hong Yu est un havre de paix et de stabilité dans une ville connue pour ses embouteillages, ses chantiers et son chaos permanent. Li, à Pékin depuis 20 ans, vit depuis quatre ans dans ce duplex dans un gratte-ciel. Il offre en abondance une denrée rare dans la capitale : « L'espace est inondé de lumière toute la journée. » Avec son ex-mari Simon et son ami décorateur Muo Ping, elle a créé un décor sobre et contemporain qui complète les vues dégagées sur Chaoyang. L'escalier transparent qui mène aux chambres semble flotter dans l'air. Les pièces sont aménagées avec quelques tableaux et objets bien choisis qui reflètent l'amour de Li pour la culture chinoise et asiatique.

Chaque objet a son histoire mais la plus belle est celle du paravent en bois sculpté de la dynastie Qing offert par un ami. Il vient de la demeure de Li Lian Ying, le célèbre dernier eunuque de la cour impériale et favori de l'impératrice douairière Cixi. Après avoir vu son lot d'intrigues et de conspirations, ce trésor de l'histoire chinoise trône désormais dans le séjour serein et moderne de Li.

LEFT ABOVE:
On the upstairs landing, a precious Qing Dynasty chair crafted from the rare huanghuali hardwood.

LEFT BELOW:
A Ming Dynasty chair and a reproduction stone Buddha from Thailand in front of a wooden screen that belonged to China's last Imperial eunuch.

RIGHT ABOVE:
The comfortably modern living room features chairs by Ligne Roset, and works by famous painter-calligrapher Yang Gang.

RIGHT BELOW:
The bathroom has white Chinese marble, and a custom-made basin. Neat blue silk-covered boxes hold toiletries.

LINKS OBEN:
Dieser wertvolle Stuhl aus der Qing-Dynastie auf der Galerie der Wohnung ist aus seltenem huanghuali-Hartholz.

LINKS UNTEN:
Vor dem Holzparavent des letzten kaiserlichen Eunuchen: ein Stuhl aus der Ming-Dynastie und die Replik einer thailändischen Buddha-Statue.

RECHTE SEITE OBEN:
Der komfortable, moderne Wohnraum mit Sitzen von Ligne Roset und Werken des bekannten Malers und Kalligrafen Yang Gang.

RECHTE SEITE UNTEN:
Das Badezimmer aus weißem chinesischem Marmor mit maßgefertigtem Waschbecken. In den mit blauer Seide bezogenen Schachteln sind Toilettenartikel verstaut.

À GAUCHE, EN HAUT :
Sur le palier de l'étage, une précieuse chaise de la dynastie Qing sculptée dans un bois rare, le huanghuali.

À GAUCHE, EN BAS :
Une chaise Ming et une copie en pierre d'un bouddha thaïlandais devant un paravent en bois ayant appartenu au dernier eunuque de la cour impériale de Chine.

PAGE DE DROITE, EN HAUT :
Le séjour moderne et confortable, avec des fauteuils Ligne Roset et des œuvres du célèbre peintre et calligraphe Yang Gang.

PAGE DE DROITE, EN BAS :
La salle de bains en marbre blanc chinois et un lavabo taillé sur mesure. Les effets de toilette sont rangés dans de belles boîtes tapissées de soie bleue.

84

KELLY LI HONG YU / CHAOYANG DISTRICT, BEIJING

RIGHT:
A cook's paradise. Li Hong Yu indulges her hobby and passion in a beautiful setting: double steel sinks, a built-in oven, microwave, and TV, luxury appliances. A Thai Buddha "kitchen god" presides, serenely, over her activities.

FOLLOWING DOUBLE PAGE:
Li Hong Yu's home altar is decorated with gold-leaf covered Thai Buddhas in different meditation poses, collected during her holidays in Bangkok.

RECHTS:
Li Hong Yu kocht leidenschaftlich gerne. Ihre tolle Küche hat zwei Edelstahlspülen, eine Mikrowelle, einen Einbauofen, einen Fernseher und Luxus-Elektrogeräte. Ein thailändischer Buddha wacht als Küchengott gelassen über das Geschehen.

FOLGENDE DOPPELSEITE:
Li Hong Yus Hausaltar. Die thailändischen Buddhas in verschiedenen Meditationsposen, die die Designerin während eines Urlaubs in Bangkok erworben hat, sind mit Blattgold bedeckt.

86

À DROITE :
Dans cette cuisine de rêve, Li Hong Yu donne libre cours à sa passion. Double évier en acier, four encastré, micro-ondes, télévision, appareils ménagers de luxe. Le dieu de la cuisine, un bouddha thaïlandais, préside sereinement aux activités de la maîtresse de maison.

DOUBLE PAGE SUIVANTE :
L'autel privé de Li Hong Yu est décoré de bouddhas dorés à la feuille dans différentes poses de méditation, qu'elle a rapportés de ses séjours à Bangkok.

KELLY LI HONG YU / CHAOYANG DISTRICT, BEIJING

Jehanne de Biolley & Harrison Liu

BEIJING

North of Beijing's Forbidden City, in three restored 17th-century pavilions, Jehanne de Biolley and her husband, Harrison Liu, have created an eclectic and intimate home. Belgian-born de Biolley is a jewellery designer with a love for Chinese stones and Asian motifs; Liu is a Chinese artist and actor who paints and designs furniture. Together they have turned this once dilapidated printing factory and school into a colorful jewel box of a house.

The compound updates the traditional Beijing courtyard house to accommodate the needs of a work-at-home family. One building is for living, another combines a kitchen and guest room, while the third houses de Biolley's workshop. In the center of the complex there is a large and homey courtyard where the couple's son Chang Ji can play among trees. The bold reds and greens of the window panes and the living room's tall lacquered columns echo the colors of de Biolley's bright necklaces and bracelets. The interior features furniture and paintings by Liu, and lovely found objects, like a gramophone and a stack of 1950s Chinese opera records that the couple discovered on the streets of Beijing.

LEFT PAGE:
Bright red and green framed window panes are a motif throughout the house.

LEFT:
Jehanne de Biolley and Harrison Liu with their son Chang Ji in the courtyard on a traditional three-wheeled cart.

LINKE SEITE:
Leuchtend rote und grüne Fensterrahmen sind das Leitmotiv des Hauses.

LINKS:
Jehanne de Biolley und Harrison Liu mit ihrem Sohn Chang Ji auf einem traditionellen Dreirad-Transporter im Innenhof.

PAGE DE GAUCHE :
On retrouve les chambranles de fenêtre rouges et verts vifs dans toute la maison.

À GAUCHE
Jehanne de Biolley et Harrison Liu avec leur fils Chang Ji dans la cour, sur un cyclopousse traditionnel.

91

Jehanne de Biolley und Ehemann Harrison Liu haben nördlich der Verbotenen Stadt in Peking aus einer zerfallenen Druckerei und Schule ein behagliches, farbiges Zuhause geschaffen. Es besteht aus drei Pavillons aus dem 17. Jahrhundert und reflektiert die Vorlieben des Paares. De Biolley – die gebürtige Belgierin ist Schmuckdesignerin – liebt chinesische Steine und asiatische Motive. Und der Künstler und Schauspieler Liu entwirft Möbel, die er bemalt.

De Biolley und Liu machten aus dem traditionellen Innenhofhaus ein modernes Wohn- und Arbeitsmodell: Eines der Pavillons ist Wohnzimmer, im zweiten befinden sich Küche und Gästezimmer, im dritten ist de Biolleys Werkstatt untergebracht. Den lauschigen Hof – an den Bäumen baumeln traditionelle Draht- und Papierlaternen – hat Chang Ji, der Sohn des Paares, zu einer Spielwiese gemacht. Grellrot und -grün bemalte Fensterrahmen, hohe, rot lackierte Säulen im Wohnraum, ein altes Grammofon, ein Stapel Platten mit chinesischen Opern – in den Straßen Pekings aufgestöbert – und die Möbel und Gemälde von Liu ergeben einen wundervoll eklektischen Mix!

Au nord de la Cité Interdite, trois pavillons du XVIIᵉ siècle ont été reconvertis par la Belge Jehanne de Biolley et son mari Harrison Liu en une demeure intime qui reflète leur personnalité. Créatrice de bijoux, de Biolley aime les gemmes chinois et les motifs asiatiques ; Liu, artiste et acteur, peint et crée des meubles. Ils ont uni leur inspiration pour transformer cette imprimerie et cette école délabrées en écrin de couleurs.

Les bâtiments ont été reliés en une version moderne de la maison pékinoise traditionnelle selon les besoins du couple qui travaille chez lui. Le premier sert pour vivre ; le second abrite la cuisine et une chambre d'amis ; le troisième est l'atelier de Jehanne. Dans la cour centrale, leur fils Chang Ji joue parmi les arbres ornés de lanternes en papier et fil de fer. Les rouges et verts des fenêtres et les colonnes laquées du séjour rappellent les créations colorées de la maîtresse de maison. Le décor éclectique est agrémenté de toiles de Liu et de jolis objets chinés dans les rues de Pékin, comme un gramophone et des piles de disques d'opéras chinois des années 1950.

PREVIOUS DOUBLE PAGE:
The living room has tall red lacquered columns, green leather sofas that date from the 1970s, and a woolen rug from Xinjiang.

LEFT PAGE:
The intricate openwork of this wooden screen is accentuated by a red and gold silk brocade lining.

RIGHT PAGE:
In an altar niche, red Buddhist prayer beads dangle above a porcelain jar that says, in Chinese, "double happiness."

VORIGE DOPPELSEITE:
Die grünen Ledersofas im Wohnzimmer mit den hohen, rot lackierten Säulen sind aus den 1970ern. Der Wollteppich stammt aus Xinjiang.

LINKE SEITE:
Die Trennwand mit aufwendig gearbeiteten Mustern wird durch den rotgoldenen Seidenbrokat zusätzlich aufgewertet.

RECHTE SEITE:
Rote buddhistische Gebetskette über einem Porzellangefäß mit der chinesischen Inschrift „Doppeltes Glück" in einer Altarnische.

DOUBLE PAGE PRÉCÉDENTE :
Dans le salon, de hautes colonnes en laque rouge, des canapés en cuir vert des années 1970 et un tapis en laine de Xinjiang.

PAGE DE GAUCHE :
Les motifs complexes de ce paravent ajouré en bois sont mis en valeur par une doublure en brocart de soie rouge et or.

PAGE DE DROITE :
Dans un autel en niche, un chapelet bouddhique rouge est suspendu au-dessus d'une jarre en porcelaine sur laquelle est écrit « double bonheur ».

JEHANNE DE BIOLLEY & HARRISON LIU / BEIJING

The big brass bed was
designed by Harrison Liu.
It is covered with silk
velvet, gold brocade, and
satin cushions.

*Das Messingbett mit
Seidensamt, Goldbrokat
und Satinkissen ist ein
Entwurf von Harrison Liu.*

*Le grand lit en laiton a été
dessiné par Harrison Liu. Il
est couvert de velours de
soie, de brocart d'or et de
coussins en satin.*

96

JEHANNE DE BIOLLEY & HARRISON LIU / BEIJING

François Maïnetti

BEIJING

"You know you are in Beijing when you are in this house," says François Maïnetti with satisfaction. Maïnetti loves to live like a local; his job with Baccarat has taken him to posts in Paris and New York. When he, his wife and four-year-old son found themselves posted to Beijing, there was no question that the family would choose a home with a strong sense of place. Through a friend, Maïnetti found the historic house in the *hutong* with its three buildings, small open courtyard, and inspiring view of the rooftops of a nearby Tibetan temple. It was perfect: there was space for Maïnetti to have a separate office in one building, and plenty of courtyard space for his son's outdoor romps.

Maïnetti ripped out the previous tenant's carpeting, modernized bathrooms and kitchen, repainted some of the walls and the moon gates in "those Chinese reds and blues you often see in paintings," and worked with Beijing artisans on custom-made furniture. With the renovation complete, la famille Maïnetti is now learning how to live in a traditional Chinese house where bedrooms and living rooms are in different buildings, separated by outdoor space.

LEFT PAGE:
Chinese table and traditional wooden benches in the courtyard of the Maïnetti family house, where lovely dinner parties are held amid the blooming dahlias.

LEFT:
A traditional moon gate flanked by kaki trees welcomes visitors to the historic courtyard home.

LINKE SEITE:
Chinesischer Tisch und traditionelle Holzstühle im Innenhof der Maïnettis. Hier finden Dinner-Partys mitten in blühenden Dahlien statt.

LINKS:
Das traditionelle Mondtor mit Kakibäumen heißt die Gäste im historischen Innenhofhaus willkommen.

PAGE DE GAUCHE :
Des tables et des bancs traditionnels en bois dans la cour, où les Maïnetti donnent des dîners charmants parmi les dahlias en fleurs.

À GAUCHE :
Une porte lune flanquée de plaqueminiers accueille les visiteurs dans la cour de la maison traditionnelle.

„Hier merkt man sofort, dass man in Peking ist", sagt François Maïnetti über sein Haus. In die chinesische Hauptstadt kam er zusammen mit seiner Frau und seinem vierjährigen Sohn durch seinen Job bei der Kristallglasmanufaktur Baccarat. Zuvor lebten die Maïnettis in Paris, dann in New York „in einem typischen Upper-West-Side-Apartment im Woody-Allen-Stil". Das historische Anwesen in einem *hutong*-Viertel fand Maïnetti durch einen Freund. Es besteht aus drei Häusern, einem kleinen Innenhof und hat eine schöne Sicht auf die Dächer eines tibetischen Tempels. Genug Platz, damit Maïnetti ein eigenes Büro in einem der Häuser einrichten konnte. Und sein Sohn liebt es, im Innenhof herumzutollen.

Maïnetti ließ vor dem Einzug die hässlichen Teppiche der früheren Besitzer herausreißen, modernisierte Badezimmer und Küche, ließ ein paar Wände und alle Mondtore in „China-Blau und -Rot, das man oft in Gemälden sieht" anmalen. Die Möbel wurden von Pekinger Handwerkern angefertigt. Nun lernen die Maïnettis die traditionelle chinesische Lebensart mit Schlaf- und Wohnräumen in getrennten Häusern kennen.

« Quand vous entrez ici, vous savez que vous êtes à Pékin », déclare François Maïnetti avec satisfaction. Il aime vivre comme les locaux. Après Paris, son travail pour Baccarat l'a envoyé à New York, où sa famille et lui habitaient dans un appartement typique du Upper West Side «semblant sorti d'un film de Woody Allen». En arrivant à Pékin avec sa femme et leur fils de quatre ans, un ami les a aidés à trouver cette maison historique dans un *hutong*, composée de trois bâtiments d'une petite cour avec une jolie vue sur les toits d'un temple tibétain. Elle était idéale, avec un bureau à part et plein d'espace à l'air libre pour l'enfant.

Maïnetti a arraché la vieille moquette, modernisé les salles de bains et la cuisine, repeint des murs et les portes lune de « ces bleus et rouges chinois qu'on voit dans les tableaux » et fait réaliser des meubles sur mesure par des artisans locaux. La restauration achevée, la petite famille apprend à vivre dans une demeure traditionnelle où les chambres et les séjours sont séparés par des cours.

PREVIOUS DOUBLE PAGE:
*Inside the beautifully
designed courtyard. The
traditional Chinese table
and benches were commis-
sioned from local artisans.*

RIGHT:
*The open-air courtyard,
seen here through the
moon gate, is the only
connection between the
house's three small
buildings.*

VORIGE DOPPELSEITE:
*Wunderschön gestalteter
Innenhof: Tisch und Stühle
wurden von lokalen Hand-
werkern angefertigt.*

RECHTS:
*Blick auf den Innenhof, der
die drei Häuser verbindet,
durch das Mondtor.*

DOUBLE PAGE PRÉCÉDENTE :
*La belle cour paysagée.
Maïnetti a fait réaliser les
tables et les chaises
chinoises par des artisans
locaux.*

À DROITE :
*La cour, vue depuis la porte
lune, est le seul lien entre
les trois petits bâtiments.*

102

FRANÇOIS MAÏNETTI / BEIJING

LEFT PAGE:
The indoor dining room, decorated with Chinese silk lamps that Maïnetti had custom made in Beijing. The family deliberately brought almost no furniture to Beijing from their Paris home.

RIGHT PAGE:
A bright red antique Tibetan rug with dragons adds color to the sitting area.

LINKE SEITE:
Das Esszimmer mit chinesischen Seidenlampen, die Maïnetti in Peking anfertigen ließ. Er nahm bewusst nur sehr wenige Möbel von Paris mit.

RECHTE SEITE:
Farbtupfen im Wohnzimmer: der antike, leuchtend rote Tibet-Teppich mit Drachenmotiv.

PAGE DE GAUCHE :
La salle à manger, ornée de lanternes en soie que Maïnetti a commandées sur mesure à des artisans chinois. Il a mis un point d'honneur à n'apporter aucun meuble de son appartement parisien.

104 PAGE DE DROITE :
Un tapis tibétain rouge ancien vif apporte de la couleur au coin salon.

LEFT ABOVE:
A Baccarat crystal Buddha, designed by Kenzo.

LEFT BELOW:
The crystal candelabras on the custom-made table are a reproduction of an original 19th-century Baccarat design.

RIGHT ABOVE:
Maïnetti designed the red lacquered doors that slide shut to hide the kitchen area.

RIGHT BELOW:
The guest bedroom is in the same building as Maïnetti's home office. The screens are made of Chinese black wood.

LINKS OBEN:
Diesen Kristall-Buddha hat Kenzo für Baccarat entworfen.

LINKS UNTEN:
Replik eines Baccarat-Designs aus dem 19. Jahrhundert: Kristallleuchter auf dem maßgefertigten Tisch.

RECHTE SEITE OBEN:
Entwurf Maïnettis: die rot lackierte Schiebetüre, die die Küche vom Wohnraum trennt.

RECHTE SEITE UNTEN:
Gästezimmer und Heimbüro sind im selben Haus untergebracht. Über dem Bett hängen Gitterdekorationen aus chinesischem Schwarzholz.

À GAUCHE, EN HAUT :
Un bouddha en cristal de Baccarat, dessiné par Kenzo.

À GAUCHE, EN BAS :
Les chandeliers en cristal sont une réplique d'un modèle de Baccarat du XIXᵉ siècle.

PAGE DE DROITE, EN HAUT :
Maïnetti a dessiné les portes en laque rouge qui coulissent pour cacher la cuisine.

PAGE DE DROITE, EN BAS :
La chambre d'amis se trouve dans le même bâtiment que le bureau de Maïnetti. Les écrans au mur sont en bois noir chinois.

FRANÇOIS MAÏNETTI / BEIJING

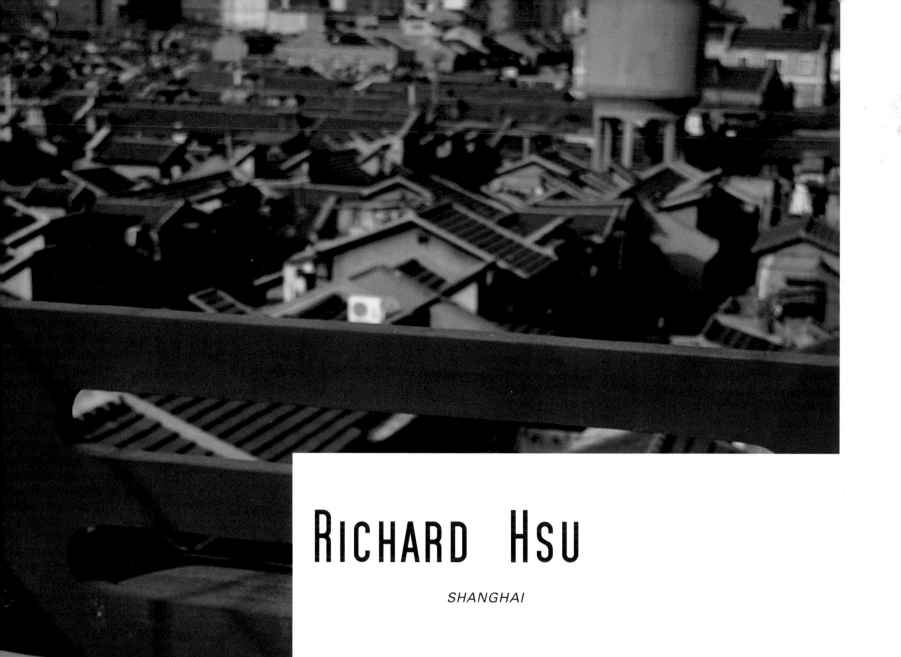

Richard Hsu

SHANGHAI

When Richard Hsu's parents come to visit him in Shanghai, they're always a bit confused. "Chinese don't understand loft living, it isn't part of the architectural tradition," he laughs. But Hsu, who left Shanghai as a child then lived all around the world, in London, New York, Tokyo, and Bangkok, has always preferred to live in open spaces. When the top floor of a converted Shanghai hardware factory (just like in London and New York, Shanghai's arts and advertising professionals are taking over the city's old industrial spaces) went up for rent, Hsu jumped at the opportunity.

Hsu, an architect, advertising consultant, and photographer (he was Richard Avedon's assistant), designed the apartment himself, taking advantage of the factory's original details – double-height ceilings, iron roof bracing. He's added luxurious touches of his own, too: the all-new bathroom sits in a transparent greenhouse on the roof. With all-around views of the gray-tiled rooftops of *shikumen*-style houses in this old Shanghai neighborhood, the loft has become a center for creative friends and business associates. "It took me a long time to find my place in Shanghai." Now he has.

111

Immer wenn Richard Hsus Eltern ihren Sohn in seinem Loft in Schanghai besuchen, schütteln sie den Kopf. „Chinesen verstehen das Konzept eines Lofts nicht", lacht Hsu, der als Kind von Schanghai wegzog und in London, New York, Tokio und Bangkok lebte. Er liebt es, in offenen Räumen zu wohnen, und als sich ihm die Möglichkeit bot, die oberste Etage einer umgebauten Fabrik in Schanghai zu mieten, zögerte er nicht lange. Wie in London und New York in den 1980ern übernehmen heute die Kreativen Schanghais die alten Industriegebäude.

Hsu, ein Architekt, Werbeberater und Fotograf (in New York war er Richard Avedons Assistent), entwarf die Pläne für sein Apartment selbst. Er nutzte bestehende Elemente wie die zweifache Deckenhöhe und die Eisenstruktur unter dem Dach und ergänzte sie mit luxuriösen Teilen. Sein brandneues Badezimmer befindet sich in einem Gewächshaus mitten auf dem Dach. Hsus Loft, von dem man auf die grauen Dächer der alten *shikumen*-Häuser sieht, ist Treffpunkt für Freunde und Geschäftspartner und der Mittelpunkt seines Lebens: „Endlich bin ich in Schanghai angekommen."

Quand les parents de Richard Hsu lui rendent visite à Shanghai, ils sont un peu déroutés. « Les Chinois ne comprennent pas le concept du loft, trop éloigné de leur tradition architecturale. » Hsu, qui a quitté Shanghai enfant et a vécu à Londres, New York, Tokyo et Bangkok, préfère les espaces ouverts. Découvrant que le dernier étage d'une ancienne usine de ferblanterie était à louer, il n'a pas hésité (comme à Londres et New York dans les années 1980, les artistes et publicitaires envahissent les vieux espaces industriels de la ville).

Architecte, consultant en publicité et photographe (il fut l'assistant de Richard Avedon à New York) Hsu a décoré l'appartement en tirant profit de ses beaux détails originaux – double hauteur sous plafond, poutrelles – et en ajoutant ses propres touches de luxe. La salle de bains se trouve dans une serre sur le toit. Avec sa vue panoramique sur les tuiles grises des *shikumen* de ce vieux quartier, le loft est devenu le point de rencontre des amis artistes et des associés de Hsu. « J'ai mis du temps à trouver ma place à Shanghai », confie-t-il. C'est désormais chose faite.

LEFT AND RIGHT PAGE:
Hsu's bedroom is located on a sleeping platform above the main level. It is accessed by a floating wooden staircase concealed behind a wall partition.

FOLLOWING DOUBLE PAGE:
Hsu's interior design is inspired by a life lived on three continents. A wooden mah-johng table and custom-built Chinese stools grace this ultra-modern kitchen.

LINKE UND RECHTE SEITE:
Hsus Schlafzimmer ist eigentlich eine Schlafplattform über dem Hauptgeschoss. Eine schwebende Treppe hinter der Trennwand führt nach oben.

FOLGENDE DOPPELSEITE:
Dass Hsu auf drei verschiedenen Kontinenten gelebt hat, sieht man der Inneneinrichtung an. In der ultramodernen Küche stehen ein traditioneller mah-jong-Tisch und maßgefertigte chinesische Stühle.

PAGES DE GAUCHE ET DE DROITE :
La chambre de Hsu est située en mezzanine. On y accède par un escalier flottant en bois caché derrière une cloison.

DOUBLE PAGE SUIVANTE :
Le décor de Hsu s'inspire de sa vie passée sur trois continents. Devant sa cuisine ultramoderne, une table de mah-johng en bois et des tabourets chinois fabriqués sur mesure.

112

In the living area, the back
panel functions as a black-
board, where Hsu's guests
can write messages and
draw pictures.

Der schwarze Raumteiler
im Wohnteil dient als Tafel.
Freunde hinterlassen hier
Nachrichten oder zeichnen
Bilder darauf.

Le coin séjour. La cloison
du fond fait office de tableau noir sur lequel les
invités de Hsu peuvent
laisser des messages et
dessiner.

LEFT ABOVE:
A traditional mask for the Chinese lion dance, xing shi, performed at the beginning of events to "wake up" good luck and ensure an auspicious outcome.

LEFT BELOW:
Richard Hsu relaxes with his dog Wolf.

RIGHT ABOVE:
The dining area, with Hsu's collection of vintage Chinese chairs. He's been collecting them for 20 years.

RIGHT BELOW:
Hsu's rooftop bathroom is enclosed on four sides by a glass greenhouse. From the tub there is a 360-degree view.

LINKS OBEN:
Eine traditionelle Maske, wie sie beim chinesischen Löwentanz xing shi getragen wird. Der Tanz wird jeweils zu Beginn einer Veranstaltung aufgeführt. Er soll Glück und Erfolg bringen.

LINKS UNTEN:
Richard Hsu entspannt sich mit seinem Hund Wolf.

RECHTE SEITE OBEN:
Hsu sammelt seit 20 Jahren Objekte wie diese antiken chinesischen Stühle in der Essecke.

RECHTE SEITE UNTEN:
Rundumsicht aus der Badewanne: Hsus Badezimmer liegt in einem vierseitig verglasten Gewächshaus auf dem Dach.

À GAUCHE, EN HAUT :
Un masque traditionnel de xing shi, la danse du lion exécutée au début d'une fête pour « réveiller » la chance et assurer une issue heureuse.

À GAUCHE, EN BAS :
Richard Hsu se détend avec son chien Wolf.

PAGE DE DROITE, EN HAUT :
La salle à manger, avec certaines des chaises anciennes que Hsu collectionne depuis vingt ans.

PAGE DE DROITE, EN BAS :
La salle de bains est protégée des quatre côtés par une serre en verre. Depuis la baignoire, on a une vue à 360°.

TENG KUN YEN

SHANGHAI

Since Taiwan-born architect and artist Teng Kun Yen moved to Shanghai ten years ago, he's become the leader of a movement to preserve his adopted city's architectural treasures. In 1997, he rehabilitated a workshop in an abandoned 1920s warehouse on the Suzhou – dozens of other creative people followed suit and soon the area was being touted as "Shanghai's Soho." (Teng's careful renovation received an honorable mention from UNESCO.)

His apartment on the Bund, where he has lived since 1998, is in a landmark building with a fascinating history: it was built in 1905, by the famous Japanese architect Hirano, to serve as the Japanese consulate in Shanghai. Although the building's name in Chinese means "Red Mansion," Teng prefers neutral colors for the interior of his open, loft-like space. Minimal furniture and simple décor allow the magnificent features of the structure – ornate ceiling moldings, unusually curved walls, and stately supporting columns – to speak for themselves. "From my window I can see the famous Pearl Tower, and the ships and boats moving along the Huang Pu River.

123

Der aus Taiwan stammende Architekt und Künstler Teng Kun Yen zog 1997 nach Schanghai. Er mietete am Suzhou-Fluss eine ehemalige Werkstätte in einem verlassenen Lagerhaus aus den 1920ern und setzte sie instand. Dutzende anderer Kreativer folgten seinem Beispiel. Die Gegend wurde bald als Soho von Schanghai bekannt und Teng als tatkräftiger Bewahrer von Architekturschätzen. Seine sorgfältige Restaurierung wurde sogar von der UNESCO gewürdigt.

In einem anderen außergewöhnlichen Gebäude befindet sich seine Wohnung. Das Haus wurde 1905 vom bekannten japanischen Architekten Hirano für das japanische Konsulat gebaut. Obwohl es den Namen „Rote Villa" trägt, setzt Teng im loftähnlichen Raum auf weiße und neutrale Töne. Die minimalistische Einrichtung überlässt den originalen Zierleisten an den Decken, den gewölbten Wänden und tragenden Säulen den großen Auftritt. Teng: „Ich habe diese großartige Architektur so gelassen, wie sie ist." Durch die Fenster hat man einen tollen Blick auf den berühmten Pearl Tower und die Schiffe, die auf dem Huang Pu auf- und abgleiten.

Depuis que l'architecte et artiste taiwanais Teng Kun Yen a emménagé à Shanghai il y a dix ans, il a pris la tête du mouvement pour la restauration des trésors architecturaux de la ville. En 1997, il a retapé un atelier dans un entrepôt abandonné des années 1920 au bord du Suzhou. Bientôt, des dizaines d'autres créatifs l'ont suivi, faisant du quartier le « Soho de Shanghai ». (L'UNESCO a salué la restauration soignée de Teng).

L'appartement où il vit depuis 1998 se trouve dans un immeuble historique sur le Bund construit en 1905 par le célèbre architecte japonais Hirano pour être le consulat du Japon. Son nom chinois signifie « maison rouge » mais, pour son espace ouvert de type loft, Teng a préféré le blanc et les tons neutres. Le décor dépouillé et le mobilier sobre laissent parler la superbe structure originale : les moulures du plafond, les murs incurvés, les colonnes majestueuses. « De ma fenêtre, je vois la célèbre Pearl Tower et les bateaux sur le Huang Pu. Depuis que j'ai emménagé ici, je n'ai rien changé. La belle architecture se suffit à elle-même. »

LEFT PAGE:
From Teng's apartment, a stunning view of the Huang Pu River and the Pearl Tower in Pudong.

RIGHT PAGE:
In his loft apartment, Teng preserved the Japanese architect's original details, like the fireplace and tall supporting columns. Although his space is large, he seldom entertains, preferring to invite a friend to share wine or tea. At night, Teng says he is "often the only human being in the building."

FOLLOWING DOUBLE PAGE:
The entrance to the apartment is through the small kitchen on the other side of the windows.

LINKE SEITE:
Spektakulärer Blick aus Tengs Wohnung auf den Fluss Huang Pu und den Pearl Tower in Pudong.

RECHTE SEITE:
Die Originalentwürfe des japanischen Architekten, wie den Kamin und die Säulen, ließ Teng stehen. Obschon die Räumlichkeiten weitläufig sind, gibt Teng selten große Partys. Er zieht es vor, seine Freunde zu einem Glas Wein oder Tee einzuladen. Nachts sei er oft ganz alleine im Gebäude, sagt er.

FOLGENDE DOPPELSEITE:
Hinter dem Fenster im Wohnraum befindet sich eine kleine Küche.

PAGE DE GAUCHE :
Depuis l'appartement, Teng a une vue superbe sur le Huang Pu et la Pearl Tower de Pudong.

PAGE DE DROITE :
Dans son loft, Teng a conservé les détails originaux de l'architecte japonais, comme la cheminée et les hautes colonnes de soutien. En dépit de l'espace, il donne rarement des réceptions, préférant recevoir un ami en tête à tête pour boire du thé ou du vin. La nuit, il dit qu'il est « le seul être humain dans l'immeuble ».

DOUBLE PAGE SUIVANTE :
Le loft. On entre par la petite cuisine de l'autre côté des fenêtres.

122

Architect Teng has two desks. This Chinese table, in the corner, is where he keeps his papers. The other desk is where he actually works.

Dieser chinesische Tisch in der Ecke benutzt Teng als Papierablage. An einem zweiten Schreibtisch arbeitet er.

L'architecte Teng a deux bureaux. Le premier, dans le coin, sert à entreposer ses papiers, le second, à travailler.

126

TENG KUN YEN / SHANGHAI

TENG KUN YEN / SHANGHAI

PIA PIERRE

SHANGHAI

Pia Pierre is a renowned French archeologist who divides her time between a feudal lord's house in Bangkok, a castle in Provence, a house in Mozambique, and this exquisite pied-à-terre in Shanghai's French Concession. Pierre, who has been coming to China since the 1980s, had always been enchanted by the faded cosmopolitanism and eclectic architecture of China's great trading city on the Huang Pu River. When she finally found her Shanghai dream house, a charming ruin on a boulevard lined with plane trees, she set about transforming it into a thing of beauty, just what you'd expect from an art collector who has been living in Asia for 30 years.

Her experience in renovating houses around the world has served her well. First, she restored the bones of this fine old structure – the dark wood details, Art-déco fireplace, marble-tiled bathrooms, hardwood floors, and fine wooden verandah grilles. Then, she filled the interior spaces sparingly with handpicked pieces of Chinese furniture and precious art objects from her years of collecting. (Lately, she has opened the house as a gallery, by appointment only.) "This place had soul," says Pierre. "And I tried to respect it."

131

Die französische Archäologin Pia Pierre pendelt zwischen verschiedenen Wohnsitzen: einem feudalen Adelshaus in Bangkok, einem Schloss in der Provence, einem Haus in Mosambik – und dieser kostbaren Wohnung in Schanghais ehemaligem französischem Konzessionsgebiet. Seit den 1980ern reist Pierre regelmäßig nach China. Die kosmopolitische Atmosphäre und eklektische Architektur der Hafenstadt am Huang-Pu-Fluss haben es ihr angetan. Als die Kunstsammlerin an einem platanengesäumten Boulevard eine Ruine fand, machte sie daraus ein Schmuckstück.

Geholfen hat ihr dabei ihre Erfahrung mit der Renovierung von Häusern auf der ganzen Welt. Pierre konzentrierte sich aufs Wesentliche: Sie restaurierte zunächst alle Elemente aus dunklem Holz wie Holzböden und Holzgitter auf der Veranda, dann den Art-déco-Kamin und die Marmor-Badezimmer dieses kostbaren, alten Gebäudes. Danach stellte sie erlesene chinesische Möbel und wertvolle Kunstobjekte aus ihrer Sammlung in die Räume. Heute dient Pierres Haus auch als Galerie (nur auf Anmeldung geöffnet). Pierre: „Ich möchte die Seele des Hauses respektieren."

Pia Pierre est une archéologue française de renom qui partage son temps entre une demeure seigneuriale à Bangkok, un château en Provence, une maison au Mozambique et cet exquis pied-à-terre dans la concession française de Shanghai. Venant en Chine depuis les années 1980, elle aime le cosmopolitisme désuet et l'architecture éclectique de la grande cité marchande au bord du Huang Pu. Après avoir déniché une charmante ruine sur un boulevard bordé de platanes, la collectionneuse d'art qui vit en Asie depuis 30 ans s'est attelée à en faire un petit bijou.

Forte de son expérience dans la rénovation de maisons au quatre coins du monde, elle a adopté une stratégie simple : restaurer les atouts de la belle structure ancienne, les détails en bois sombre, la cheminée Art Déco, les salles de bains en marbre, les parquets et les grilles de la véranda. Puis elle l'a décorée de meubles chinois soigneusement choisis et d'objets d'art de sa collection. (On peut désormais visiter sur rendez-vous sa maison qui fait aussi galerie). « Cet endroit a une âme, j'ai tenté de la respecter », explique Pia.

LEFT PAGE:
In the entranceway, a Ming Dynasty calligraphy panel next to a Japanese sake jar.

RIGHT PAGE:
A Qing Dynasty table and Chinese scroll adorn a niche.

LINKE SEITE:
Im Flur lehnt an der Wand eine Tafel mit Kalligrafien aus der Ming-Dynastie neben einem japanischen Sake-Gefäß.

RECHTE SEITE:
Nischendekor: Chinesische Hängerolle über einem Tisch aus der Qing-Dynastie

PAGE DE GAUCHE :
Dans l'entrée, un panneau calligraphié de la période Ming est appuyé contre le mur, près d'une jarre à saké japonaise.

PAGE DE DROITE :
Dans une niche, un rouleau chinois derrière une table de la dynastie Qing.

132

Pierre's double-sized living room has its original Art-déco marble fireplace, accentuated by a large scroll with the Chinese character for "blessings."

Pierres Wohnraum besteht aus zwei Zimmern und verfügt über einen originalen Art-déco-Kamin aus Marmor. Darüber hängt eine Hängerolle mit dem chinesischen Schriftzeichen für „Segnungen".

Dans le grand séjour, au-dessus de la cheminée en marbre Art Déco, un grand rouleau orné de l'idéogramme chinois signifiant « bénédictions ».

134

Pearl Lam

SHANGHAI

Pearl Lam's Shanghai apartment is everything you'd expect the home of an international art diva to be: unconventional and filled with furniture, paintings, and objects from the hottest designers and artists in China. "I don't like limitations," says Lam. "I want to display as much of my collection in my home as I can." With 1,000 square meters of space, there's a lot of room for Lam's collection, which encompasses everything from paintings by artist friends like He Jia, to objects from XYZ Design, the company she founded to showcase talented new Chinese designers. Despite the abundance of styles, Lam's personality pulls them all together.

Lam's talent for harmonizing contrasts isn't limited to art objects. Her apartment on the 22nd floor of a new building in Shanghai's French Concession has become a place where the city's creative elite mixes with Lam's friends and associates from all over the world. They gather in her dining room that can seat 66 people, or on four big balconies, at cocktail parties. Be forewarned: the hostess insists that the conversation be challenging. Says Lam: "I am only interested in utter newness."

137

Pearl Lams Schanghaier Wohnung ist genau so, wie man es von einer Kunst-Diva erwartet: unkonventionell, gewagt, eigenwillig. Und natürlich ist sie voller Möbel, Bilder und Objekte der in China angesagtesten Designer und Künstler. „Die Kunst steht bei mir im Mittelpunkt, und ich möchte so viel wie möglich von meiner Sammlung zeigen", erklärt Lam. Mit 1000 Quadratmetern Wohnfläche ein einfaches Versprechen! In Lams außergewöhnlicher und großer Sammlung findet man so ziemlich alles – von Bildern befreundeter Künstler wie He Jia bis hin zu Objekten von XYZ Design, einer Firma, die Lam zur Förderung junger chinesischer Design-Talente gegründet hat.

Lams Wohnung im 22. Geschoss eines neuen Gebäudes in Schanghais ehemaligem französischem Konzessionsgebiet ist nicht nur Ausstellungsraum, sondern auch Treffpunkt der kreativen Elite der Stadt, die Lam mit ihren Freunden und Geschäftspartnern aus aller Welt zusammenbringt. Etwa zum Dinner an ihrem riesigen Esstisch, an dem 66 Personen Platz finden, oder zur Cocktailparty auf einer ihrer vier großen Terrassen.

L'appartement de Pearl Lam est à l'image de cette diva internationale du monde de l'art : extravagant, anticonformiste et rempli de meubles, tableaux et objets des plus grands créateurs et artistes du moment. « Je n'aime pas les limites », explique-t-elle. « Je veux montrer le plus de pièces possibles. Toutes mes résidences sont des concentrés d'art. » Ses 1000 mètres carré suffisent à peine à contenir sa collection, incluant aussi bien des toiles d'amis comme He Jia que des objets de XYZ Design, sa compagnie fondée pour promouvoir de jeunes designers. La personnalité de la maîtresse de maison harmonise le mélange contrasté de styles, formes et couleurs. « Je suis contradictoire, alors chez moi ça marche. »

L'appartement, au 22e étage d'une tour dans la concession française, est devenu le lieu où l'élite créative de Shanghai côtoie les amis et associés cosmopolites de Lam. Ils se réunissent dans la salle à manger, dont la table peut accueillir 66 personnes, ou sur les quatre grands balcons. Mais soyez prévenu : l'hôtesse exige que la conversation soit à la hauteur de son intérieur. « Seul le totalement nouveau m'intéresse. »

RIGHT:
Lam's dazzling formal dining room has a 15-meter-long table, with a blue glass top and brass-colored base. The feathered chandelier in the center is from Lam's XYZ Design. The candelabra are by designer Franck Evennou.

FOLLOWING DOUBLE PAGE:
After dinner, Lam's guests repair to this "coffee room" for drinks and conversation. A vintage 1960s plastic bubble chair shares the spotlight with an 18th-century Chinese opium bed covered with zebra-print silk. The sculpture of Mao's jacket is by Sui Jiangou.

RECHTS:
Beeindruckende 15 Meter lang ist der Esstisch mit blauen Glasplatten, messingfarbenem Gestell und deliriöser Wirkung. Die mit Federn geschmückten Leuchter über dem Tisch sind von XYZ Design, Pearl Lams Firma, die silbernen Kerzenständer hat Franck Evennou entworfen.

FOLGENDE DOPPELSEITE:
Nach dem Dinner ziehen sich die Gäste in den Salon zurück und unterhalten sich bei Drinks. Der „Bubble Chair" ist ein Original aus den 1960ern und das chinesische Opium-Bett mit rosa Zebraprint-Seidenbezug stammt aus dem 18. Jahrhundert. Die Skulptur einer Mao-Jacke ist von Sui Jiangou.

À DROITE :
L'éblouissante salle à manger de Lam dont la table mesure 15 m de long. Son plateau est en verre bleu sur un support couleur cuivre. Le lustre bordé de plumes au centre provient de la société de Lam, XYZ Design. Les chandeliers sont signés Franck Evennou.

DOUBLE PAGE SUIVANTE :
Après le dîner, les convives se retirent dans le « salon de café » pour discuter autour d'un verre. Un fauteuil « bulle » des années 1960 côtoie un lit à opium chinois du XVIIIe siècle tapissé d'une soierie imprimée d'un motif en peau de zèbre. La sculpture de la veste de Mao est de Sui Jiangou.

138

LEFT ABOVE:
An ante-room: Lam's open spaces are divided with intricately carved wooden and aluminum hanging screens by designer Danny Lane.

LEFT BELOW:
Lam had these white chairs from XYZ Design specially painted with polka dots. The painting is by He Jia.

RIGHT ABOVE AND BELOW:
In an alcove, two sculptures by Chinese artist Luo Xu: "East Venus No. 1" and "East Venus No. 2".

FOLLOWING DOUBLE PAGE:
"I have respect for history but no reverence for it," says Lam. Here in an anteroom, she's placed a Ming Dynasty antique wooden Buddha beside a contemporary glass table by Danny Lane, an acid-green glass bowl by Prague-born designer Bořek Šípek, and a modern sofa by Mattia Bonetti, the "Press Couch", with custom fabric inspired by Chinese periodicals.

LINKE SEITE OBEN:
Schaffung eines Vorzimmers: aufwendig geschnitzte Hängewände aus Holz und Aluminium von Designer Danny Lane teilen den offenen Raum ab.

LINKE SEITE UNTEN:
Die weißen Stühle sind von XYZ Design. Lam hat sie mit Tupfen bemalen lassen. Das Bild an der Wand stammt von He Jia.

RECHTS OBEN UND UNTEN:
Die Skulpturen „Ost-Venus Nr. 1" und „Ost-Venus Nr. 2" hat der chinesische Künstler Luo Xu geschaffen.

FOLGENDE DOPPELSEITE:
Im Vorzimmer: ein antiker Holz-Buddha aus der Ming-Dynastie, daneben ein moderner Glastisch, entworfen von Danny Lane und eine giftgrüne Glasschale des Prager Designers Bořek Šípek: „Ich mag Historisches, lasse es aber nicht dominieren." Die „Press Couch" von Mattia Bonetti wurde von chinesischen Magazinen inspiriert.

PAGE DE GAUCHE, EN HAUT :
Une antichambre. Les espaces ouverts de l'appartement sont séparés par des écrans en bois et aluminium ouvragés suspendus au plafond, des créations de Danny Lane.

PAGE DE GAUCHE, EN BAS :
Les fauteuils blancs sont de XYZ Design. Lam a demandé à quelqu'un de les lui peindre avec des pois de couleurs. La peinture au mur est de He Jia.

À DROITE, EN HAUT ET EN BAS :
Dans une alcôve, deux sculptures de l'artiste chinois Luo Xu : « Vénus de l'Est n°1 » et « Vénus de l'Est n°2 ».

DOUBLE PAGE SUIVANTE :
« Je respecte l'histoire sans la vénérer », dit Lam. Dans cette antichambre, elle a placé un bouddha en bois ancien de la dynastie Ming près d'une table basse en verre de Danny Lane, d'une coupe en cristal vert acidulé du designer pragois Bořek Šípek et d'un canapé moderne de Mattia Bonetti, le « divan de la presse », tapissé d'un tissu imprimé s'inspirant de revues chinoises.

PEARL LAM / SHANGHAI

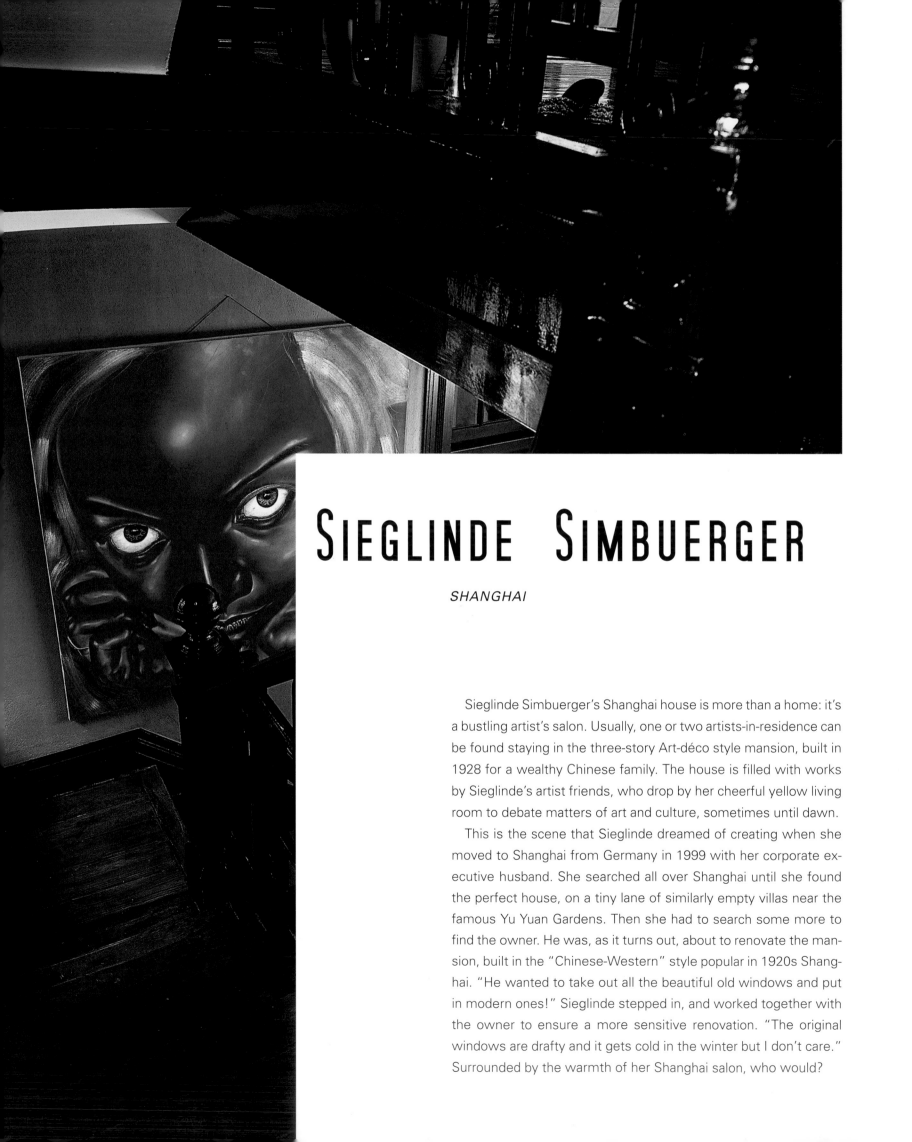

Sieglinde Simbuerger

SHANGHAI

Sieglinde Simbuerger's Shanghai house is more than a home: it's a bustling artist's salon. Usually, one or two artists-in-residence can be found staying in the three-story Art-déco style mansion, built in 1928 for a wealthy Chinese family. The house is filled with works by Sieglinde's artist friends, who drop by her cheerful yellow living room to debate matters of art and culture, sometimes until dawn.

This is the scene that Sieglinde dreamed of creating when she moved to Shanghai from Germany in 1999 with her corporate executive husband. She searched all over Shanghai until she found the perfect house, on a tiny lane of similarly empty villas near the famous Yu Yuan Gardens. Then she had to search some more to find the owner. He was, as it turns out, about to renovate the mansion, built in the "Chinese-Western" style popular in 1920s Shanghai. "He wanted to take out all the beautiful old windows and put in modern ones!" Sieglinde stepped in, and worked together with the owner to ensure a more sensitive renovation. "The original windows are drafty and it gets cold in the winter but I don't care." Surrounded by the warmth of her Shanghai salon, who would?

LEFT PAGE:
*The mahogany staircase
in the three-story 1920s
Shanghai mansion.*

RIGHT:
*Sieglinde Simbuerger,
photographed in her Shanghai sitting room.*

LINKE SEITE:
*Die Mahagoni-Treppe in der
dreigeschossigen Schang-
haier Villa aus den 1920ern.*

RECHTS:
*Sieglinde Simbuerger in
ihrem Wohnzimmer.*

PAGE DE GAUCHE :
*L'escalier en acajou de la
villa des années 1920 relie
les trois étages.*

À DROITE :
*Sieglinde Simbuerger,
photographiée dans son
petit salon de Shanghai.*

147

Sieglinde Simbuergers Haus in Schanghai ist nicht nur ihr Zuhau-se, sondern auch ein Künstlersalon. In der dreigeschossigen Art déco Villa von 1928 sind stets ein oder zwei Künstler zu Gast. Im gelben Salon wird oft bis in die frühen Morgenstunden über Kunst und Kultur diskutiert. Die Villa ist zum Bersten gefüllt mit Gemäl-den und Skulpturen, Werke ihrer Künstlerfreunde.

Sieglinde zog mit ihrem Gatten, einem Geschäftsmann, 1999 von Deutschland nach Schanghai. Bereits bei ihrer Ankunft träum-te sie von einem Künstlerhaus und klapperte ganz Schanghai ab, bis sie ein geeignetes Haus gefunden hatte. Sie entdeckte es in der Nähe des berühmten Yu-Yuan-Gartens in einer Reihe leer ste-hender Villen im chinesisch-westlichen Stil der 1920er. Es dauerte etwas, bis sie den Besitzer ausfindig machen konnte. Dieser plan-te bereits eine Renovierung und wollte „die schönen alten Fenster durch neue ersetzen!" Sieglinde überzeugte ihn von einer sanften Renovierung. „Dass im Winter ein kalter Wind durch die alten Fenster zieht, ist mir egal." Bei der Wärme, die ihr Salon aus-strahlt, gut zu verstehen.

L'adresse de Sieglinde Simbuerger est plus qu'une simple mai-son, c'est un salon d'artistes. On en trouve toujours un ou deux en résidence dans sa villa Art Déco de trois étages, construite en 1928 pour une riche famille de commerçants dans le style « chi-nois occidental » alors en vogue. Elle est pleine à craquer de ta-bleaux et de sculptures des amis de la maîtresse de maison qui passent la voir dans son joyeux salon jaune pour discuter art et culture, parfois jusqu'à l'aube.

Sieglinde en rêvait. Quand elle est arrivée d'Allemagne en 1999 avec son mari dirigeant d'entreprise, elle s'est mise en quête dans tout Shanghai de la maison idéale, qu'elle a découverte dans une petite allée bordée d'autres villas désertes près des célèbres jar-dins Yu Yuan. Le propriétaire, une fois débusqué, voulait la réno-ver. « Il allait remplacer les belles fenêtres anciennes par des mo-dernes ! » s'indigne Sieglinde. Elle a collaboré avec lui à une restauration plus respectueuse. « Il y a des courants d'air et il fait froid l'hiver mais peu m'importe. » Effectivement, dans l'atmos-phère chaleureuse de son salon, qui s'en soucie ?

LEFT:
Sieglinde's house looks down on an old Shanghai neighborhood of shikumen-style traditional houses. There's a Confucian temple nearby.

RIGHT ABOVE:
The exterior of the house, with its Art-déco details.

RIGHT BELOW:
On the mahogany staircase, every inch of wall-space is hung with friends' paintings.

LINKE SEITE:
Blick auf die Dächer von traditionellen shikumen-Häusern in dem alten Schanghaier Viertel. In der Nähe steht auch ein Konfuzius-Tempel.

RECHTS OBEN:
Art-déco-Verzierungen an der Fassade der Villa.

RECHTS UNTEN:
Auf der Mahagoni-Treppe. Jeder Zentimeter der Wand ist mit Werken, die Freunde gestaltet haben, bedeckt.

PAGE DE GAUCHE :
La villa domine un vieux quartier de Shanghai avec ses shikumen traditionnels. Tout à côté se trouve un temple confucianiste.

À DROITE, EN HAUT :
La façade, avec ses détails Art Déco.

À DROITE, EN BAS :
Dans l'escalier en acajou, les murs sont tapissés de toiles d'amis.

SIEGLINDE SIMBUERGER / SHANGHAI

LEFT ABOVE:
The living room has original wood-framed bay windows that look onto the garden.

LEFT BELOW:
Another view of Sieglinde's cozy living room. She bought all the vintage furniture in Shanghai antique shops and second-hand markets.

RIGHT ABOVE:
Sieglinde bought her Tiffany-style lamps from the owner of a local lamp factory. The lacquer coffee table is Qing Dynasty.

RIGHT BELOW:
The guest bedroom, painted in Sieglinde's favorite color yellow, often hosts "artists in residence".

LINKS OBEN:
Holzgerahmte Original-Erkerfenster im Wohnzimmer mit Blick auf den Garten.

LINKS UNTEN:
Die Vintage-Möbel im behaglichen gelben Salon hat Sieglinde in Antiquitäten- und Secondhand-Geschäften aufgestöbert.

RECHTE SEITE OBEN:
Die Tiffany-Lampen fand Sieglinde bei einem Lampenhersteller vor Ort; der rot lackierte Tisch stammt aus der Qing-Dynastie.

RECHTE SEITE UNTEN:
Die Wände im Gästezimmer sind gelb, Sieglindes Lieblingsfarbe. Hier übernachten oft befreundete Künstler.

À GAUCHE, EN HAUT :
Dans le salon, les bay-windows d'origine donnent sur le jardin.

À GAUCHE, EN BAS :
Une autre vue du salon douillet. Sieglinde a acheté tous ses meubles anciens chez des antiquaires et des brocanteurs de Shanghai.

PAGE DE DROITE, EN HAUT :
Sieglinde a acheté ses lampes de style Tiffany au propriétaire d'une fabrique locale. La table basse en laque date de la dynastie Qing.

PAGE DE DROITE, EN BAS :
La chambre d'amis jaune, la couleur préférée de Sieglinde, accueille souvent des artistes « en résidence ».

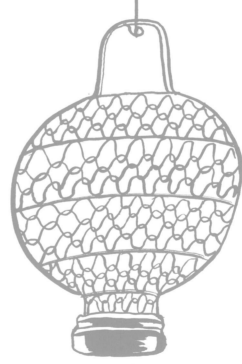

SIEGLINDE SIMBUERGER / SHANGHAI

BAO YIFENG

SHANGHAI

Bao Yifeng is a fixture of the Shanghai nightlife scene. His company, Liquid Element, does event planning and PR for luxury brands and is known for throwing the best parties in the city. Naturally, Bao has a million friends from all over China and the world; the luckiest friends are the ones Bao invites to stay in this three-story lane house in Shanghai's ultra-hot XuHui District (by the old French Concession). Bao himself lives in a similar house, just a five minute walk away.

Bao's private guesthouse is fitted throughout in classic 1920s Shanghai Art Deco furniture, one of his passions – he's collected odds and ends from antique markets all over China. Intense greens and fuschias dominate the color scheme, an influence from his stint working at David Tang's China Club in Hong Kong. "I was involved in the catalogue shooting with Gong Li for Shanghai Tang in 1996. The striking greens and yellows made a strong impression on me." Bao Yifeng's eclectic, funky, retro-Shanghai chic is a cradle for the city's rebirth of cool. "My house is old meets new, Art-déco meets contemporary, classic and modern."

155

LEFT PAGE:
In Bao Yifeng's sitting room, this vintage Mao Zedong wall banner once hung in a Chinese elementary school.

LEFT:
On the coffee table, a Chinese warrior figure wears a green Mao jacket. Bao found the piece in a Beijing shop called Dara.

LINKE SEITE:
Das Vintage-Mao-Zedong-Poster in Baos Wohnzimmer stammt aus einer chinesischen Grundschule.

LINKS:
Die Figur auf dem Couchtisch stellt einen chinesischen Krieger dar, der eine knallgrüne Mao-Jacke trägt. Bao fand sie bei Dara, einem Geschäft in Peking.

PAGE DE GAUCHE :
Dans le petit salon, le placard rétro représentant Mao Tsê-Tung se trouvait autrefois dans une école élémentaire.

À GAUCHE :
Sur la table basse, une statuette de guerrier chinois portant une veste mao verte. Bao l'a trouvée chez Dara, une boutique de Pékin.

Bao Yifeng: Dieser Name ist eine feste Größe im Schanghaier Nachtleben. Der Besitzer von Liquid Element, eine Event- und PR-Firma, die auf Luxusmarken spezialisiert ist, organisiert die coolsten Partys der Stadt. Für seine zahlreichen Freunde hat Yifeng im schicken Gassen-Viertel XuHui ein dreigeschossiges Gästehaus umgebaut. Er selbst lebt fünf Gehminuten entfernt in einem ähnlichen Gebäude.

Im Gästehaus dominiert der Schanghaier Art déco der 1920er. Die Einrichtungsstücke hat Bao auf Antiquitätenmärkten in ganz China aufgestöbert, und seine Vorliebe für Bonbonfarben hat er bei David Tangs Hongkonger China Club abgeguckt, für den er früher gearbeitet hat: „1996 wirkte ich beim Fotoshooting für den Katalog von Shanghai Tang mit Gong Li mit und war von dem typischen Leuchtgrün, Orange und Fuchsia total begeistert." Der eklektische Schanghaier Retro-Schick Baos passt perfekt zur Aufbruchstimmung, die in der Stadt herrscht: „In meinem Haus trifft Neues auf Altes, Art déco auf Zeitgenössisches, Klassisches auf Modernes."

Bao Yifeng est une personnalité de la Shanghai nocturne. Sa société Liquid Element, qui organise des événements et s'occupe des relations publiques de marques de luxe, est connue pour donner les meilleures fêtes de la ville. Naturellement, Bao a un million d'amis en Chine et dans le monde entier. Les plus chanceux sont ceux qu'il invite dans sa maison de trois étages dans le quartier ultra branché de XuHui (près de la concession française). Lui-même habite dans une autre demeure similaire, à cinq minutes à pied.

Sa maison d'amis est décorée de meubles Art Déco de Shanghai, une de ses passions, qu'il a chinés chez des antiquaires de toute la Chine. Les verts et les fuchsias intenses dominent la palette de couleur, une influence de son passage au China Club de David Tang à Hong-Kong. «J'ai travaillé sur les photos de Gong Li pour le catalogue de Shanghai Tang en 1996. J'ai été frappé par les verts, les jaunes et les orange.» Son style rétro chic éclectique et branché incarne la renaissance du cool en ville. «J'ai marié le vieux et le neuf, l'Art Déco et le contemporain, l'ancien et le moderne. J'aime les contrastes.»

The main sitting room of
Bao Yifeng's guesthouse.
The acid-green color of the
upholstery was inspired by
Shanghai Tang.

Die leuchtend grüne
Farbe des Sofas im großen
Wohnzimmer des Gäste-
hauses ist durch das Label
Shanghai Tang inspiriert.

Le salon principal de la
maison d'amis. Le vert
acidulé du canapé et des
fauteuils a été inspiré par
Shanghai Tang.

156

LEFT PAGE:
The narrow lane that leads to Bao's guesthouse, in Shanghai's XuHui District, bustling with vendors and carts.

RIGHT PAGE:
Bao chose the cream and gold wallpaper to give a colonial feeling to the study. He found the pen-holder (shaped like a clock tower on the Bund) in a Shanghai secondhand shop.

LINKE SEITE:
Diese schmale, von Straßenhändlern gesäumte Gasse im Schanghaier Viertel XuHui führt zu Baos Gästehaus.

RECHTE SEITE:
Creme- und goldfarbene Tapeten passen zum Kolonial-Look des Studier-zimmers. Der Federhalter in der Form eines Uhren-turms stammt aus einem Schanghaier Secondhand-shop im Bund-Viertel.

PAGE DE GAUCHE :
La ruelle étroite qui mène à la maison d'amis de Bao, dans le quartier XuHui, est toujours pleine de carrioles et de marchands ambulants.

158

PAGE DE DROITE :
Bao a choisi le papier peint beige et or pour don-ner une ambiance coloniale au bureau. Il a trouvé support de porte-plume (représentant un des clochers qui bordent le Bund) chez un brocanteur de Shanghai.

MIAN MIAN

SHANGHAI

Shanghai writer Mian Mian is one of the most controversial figures of her generation in China. Her brave and outspoken novels break taboos, and venture into areas where "respectable" Chinese writers have long feared to tread. Think: sex, drugs, rock and roll. Young Chinese women speak her name with the reverence usually reserved for pop stars. Mian Mian's books sell millions of copies worldwide.

Her rented Shanghai apartment in the North Bund Garden area is as unconventional as you'd expect. Actually, it is not Mian Mian's home; it is a project entitled "Every Good Kid Deserves Candy," after one of her collections of short stories. She explains: "The apartment is not for me: it is a playroom, a studio, an office, a showroom." Inside the sparsely furnished space are works of art created by some of her already-famous artist friends. But Mian Mian's passion is finding "art kids of the future" – creative souls who are helping shape the New Shanghai. She exhibits their works in her 140-square-meter pad with its terrific skyscraper view and silver-foil wrapped walls. "My art-apartments are the future."

161

Die Schriftstellerin Mian Mian ist eine der umstrittensten Persönlichkeiten Chinas. Mit ihren Romanen bricht sie Tabus und schreibt unbefangen über Sex, Drogen und Rock and Roll. Themen, an die sich etablierte Schriftsteller bisher kaum herantrauten. Kein Wunder, dass sie in China von der jungen Frauengeneration bewundert wird wie ein Popstar. Weltweit verkaufen sich ihre Bücher millionenfach.

Ihre Mietwohnung in der Nähe des Nord-Bund-Gartens ist genauso unkonventionell wie sie selbst. Eigentlich ist es nicht ihr Zuhause, sondern ein Kunstprojekt mit dem Titel „Every Good Kid Deserves Candy", benannt nach ihrer Kurzgeschichtensammlung. Es ist Spielzimmer, Studio, Büro und Showroom zugleich. Im spärlich möblierten Raum stehen überall Werke befreundeter, mittlerweile bekannter Künstler. Am liebsten entdeckt Mian Mian aber junge Künstler mit Potenzial, solche die das neue Schanghai mitprägen. Deren Werke stellt sie in ihrer 140 Quadratmeter großen, alufolientapezierten Bleibe mit umwerfender Aussicht auf die Wolkenkratzer aus: „Meine Kunst-Apartments sind die Zukunft."

Mian Mian est l'une des écrivaines les plus sulfureuses de sa génération. Ses romans brisent les tabous et s'aventurent là où les auteurs chinois « respectables » n'osent pas aller : *sex, drugs and rock'n roll*. Les Chinoises de 30 et 40 ans prononcent son nom avec la révérence réservée aux idoles pop. Ses livres sont vendus par millions dans le monde entier.

Les 140 mètres carrés qu'elle loue près de North Bund Garden sont aussi originaux qu'elle, avec des murs en papier alu et une vue superbe sur les gratte-ciels. Elle n'y vit pas, c'est un projet intitulé « Les enfants sages méritent des bonbons », d'après un recueil de ses nouvelles. « C'est une salle de jeux, un atelier, un showroom », explique-t-elle. L'espace dépouillé abrite des œuvres d'amis déjà célèbres mais sa passion est de découvrir les « petits artistes du futur », des créatifs qui façonneront le nouveau Shanghai. Celle qui a ébranlé les fondements de la littérature chinoise et s'en prend à présent aux barricades de l'art déclare : « Les appartements d'art de Mian Mian sont l'avenir. Quand elle bouge, une porte s'ouvre. »

LEFT ABOVE:
A mini-skirted Mian Mian in her Shanghai art-apartment.

LEFT BELOW:
Silver doors lead to one of the apartment's two recently renovated bathrooms. She rents the apartment from a friend, architect Zhuang Jan.

RIGHT ABOVE:
Mian Mian's covered most of her apartment walls with shiny silver paper. "It makes the place look simple, and it is like a candy wrapper." The bicycle sculpture is by artist Shi Jin Dian.

RIGHT BELOW:
Mian Mian's first art-apartment exhibit was this three-panel painting.

LINKS OBEN:
Mian Mian in ihrem Schanghaier Apartment.

LINKS UNTEN:
Hinter versilberten Türen liegt eines der beiden renovierten Badezimmer. Mian Mian hat das Apartment von dem befreundeten Architekten Zhuang Jan gemietet.

RECHTE SEITE OBEN:
Fast alle Wände in Mian Mians Apartment sind mit glänzender Folie tapeziert: „Es verleiht den Räumen eine Einfachheit und sieht aus wie Bonbonpapier." Die Fahrrad-Skulptur stammt von Shi Jin Dian.

RECHTE SEITE UNTEN:
Das Triptychon war das erste Kunstwerk, das Mian Mian in ihrem Kunst-Apartment ausstellte.

À GAUCHE, EN HAUT :
Mian Mian en minijupe dans son appartement d'art.

À GAUCHE, EN BAS :
Des portes argentées mènent aux deux salles de bains récemment refaites. Mian Mian loue l'appartement d'un ami, l'architecte Zhuang Jan.

PAGE DE DROITE, EN HAUT :
Mian Mian a tapissé pratiquement tout l'appartement de papier aluminium. « Ça donne une allure simple, comme l'emballage d'un bonbon. » La sculpture bicyclette est de l'artiste Shi Jin Dian.

PAGE DE DROITE, EN BAS :
Ce triptyque fut la première pièce exposée dans l'appartement d'art.

MIAN MIAN / SHANGHAI

Mian Mian's place has no lamps: after dark she entertains guests by the "plastic, fantastic" light of Shanghai's iconic Pearl Tower. "We only use lighting boxes by Zhao Yao and the (ambient) lights from the Bund. So people talk in near-darkness, with little silver shining lights. Very interesting."

Lampen findet man in Mian Mians Apartment keine. Die Gäste unterhalten sich abends praktisch im Dunkeln. Einzige Lichtquellen: das knallige Licht des legendären Schanghaier Pearl Towers, das Straßenlicht des Bund-Viertels, Reflektionen auf dem Silberpapier und die Lichtboxen des Künstlers Zhao Yao.

Il n'y a pas de lampes dans l'appartement. La nuit tombée, Mian Mian reçoit ses invités à la lueur «plastique, fantastique» de la célèbre Pearl Tower de Shanghai. «Nous n'utilisons que des caissons lumineux de Zhao Yao et les lumières provenant du Bund, si bien que les gens sont dans une pénombre ponctuée de petites lueurs argentées. Très intéressant.»

164

FUCHUN RESORT

HANGZHOU

Hangzhou, in Zhejiang Province, may be the most beautiful city in China. It is built around a man-made lake, the blue Xi Hu, which has inspired poets and painters for centuries. Nestled beside the green Fuchun Mountains, terraced with tea plantations, Hangzhou is a fantasy of architectural wonders from all eras. There are ancient pagodas that date from the Song Dynasty in the 13th century, when Hangzhou was the capital of China and the most populous city on earth. There are also lovely 19th- and early 20th-century villas, vacation houses for wealthy families from Beijing and Shanghai. Almost untouched by the ravages of time, Hangzhou is where the Chinese go when they need to unwind.

The Fuchun Resort is the ultimate in Hangzhou retreats. Here, in the shadow of the mountains, guests may stay in luxurious rooms or in one of the four-room villas, each with its own private pool. Traditional art objects and furniture stand alongside casual chairs and sofas. An 18-hole golf course is one of the resort's attractions, but Fuchun's sweetest delight is a cup of the prized "Longjing" or "Dragon Well" green tea from the resort's own plantation.

PREVIOUS DOUBLE PAGE:
The magical view of bridges and pagodas overlooking the Grand Canal in Hangzhou.

LEFT PAGE:
Traditional objects, like this old Song Dynasty Buddha figure, decorate the common spaces.

LEFT:
The entrance to one of Fuchun's free-standing private villas.

VORIGE DOPPELSEITE:
Blick auf Brücken und Pagoden über dem Kaiserkanal in Hangzhou.

LINKE SEITE:
Die Buddha-Statue stammt aus der Song-Dynastie.

LINKS:
Eingang zu einer der frei stehenden Privatvillen.

DOUBLE PAGE PRÉCÉDENTE :
La vue magique sur les ponts et les pagodes du Grand canal à Hangzhou.

PAGE DE GAUCHE :
Des objets traditionnels, comme cet ancien bouddha datant de la dynastie Song, décorent les espaces communs.

À GAUCHE :
L'entrée de l'une des villas privées du Fuchun Resort.

Die wohl schönste Stadt Chinas, Hangzhou in der Provinz Zhejiang, liegt am künstlich angelegten Xi-Hu See und am Fuß der grünen, mit Teeplantagen terrassierten Berge von Fuchun. Pagoden der Song-Dynastie aus dem 13. Jahrhundert sind Zeugen einer großen Vergangenheit: Hangzhou war zu jener Zeit die Hauptstadt Chinas und die größte Stadt der Welt. Schön sind auch die reizenden Villen aus dem 19. und frühen 20. Jahrhundert, heute Ferienhäuser für reiche Familien aus Peking und Schanghai. In die Idylle von Hangzhou ziehen sich die Chinesen zurück, um der Alltagshektik zu entfliehen und sich ihrer kulturellen und spirituellen Wurzeln zu besinnen.

Das exklusivste Refugium ist das Fuchun Resort mit einer 18-Loch-Golfanlage, luxuriösen Gästezimmern und 4-Zimmer-Villen, die jeweils über einen eigenen Pool verfügen. Das Interieur mit traditionellen Objekten und Möbeln zeugt vom glanzvollen Stil der Song-Dynastie und ist gleichzeitig komfortabel modern. Das schönste Vergnügen: der Genuss einer Tasse edlen „Longjing"- oder „Dragon Well"-Grüntee von der hauseigenen Plantage.

Hangzhou, dans la province de Zhejiang, doit être la plus belle ville de Chine. Nichée au pied des monts Fuchun, elle entoure le Xi Hu, un lac artificiel qui inspire les poètes et les peintres depuis des siècles. Elle abrite des joyaux architecturaux de toutes les époques : pagodes du XIIIᵉ siècle (quand la ville, alors la plus peuplée du monde, était la capitale de la dynastie Song) ; belles villas du XIXᵉ et du début du XXᵉ siècle des riches familles de Pékin et de Shanghai (à deux heures de route). Épargnée par les ravages du temps, des guerres et de l'urbanisation, les Chinois viennent s'y ressourcer et retrouver leurs racines culturelles et spirituelles.

Au Fuchun Resort, la magnificence des Song a été modernisée pour accueillir le voyageur exigeant. À l'ombre des plantations de thé en terrasses, on peut opter pour une chambre luxueuse ou une des villas équipée de sa piscine privée. Les objets d'art et le mobilier ancien côtoient les fauteuils et canapés douillets. Le golf de 18 trous est très prisé mais le vrai trésor de Fuchun, c'est une tasse de son précieux « Longjing », le thé vert « puits du Dragon ».

LEFT ABOVE:
A Song Dynasty reclining Buddha figure and wooden paneling decorate the club-house lounge of Fuchun Resort.

LEFT BELOW:
The clubhouse lounge serves fine tea, grown in the resort's own plantation.

RIGHT ABOVE:
A view of the high-ceilinged dining room, with wooden paneling and beams.

RIGHT BELOW:
The sitting area in one of the deluxe private villas.

LINKE SEITE OBEN:
Die Lounge des Klub-hauses mit liegender Buddha-Figur aus der Song-Dynastie und dekorativer Wandvertäfelung.

LINKE SEITE UNTEN:
Klubhaus-Lounge: Hier wird edler Tee von der haus-eigenen Plantage serviert.

RECHTS OBEN:
Blick auf das Esszimmer mit hohen Decken, Holz-paneelen und -balken.

RECHTS UNTEN:
Wohnecke in einer der Deluxe-Privatvillen.

PAGE DE GAUCHE, EN HAUT :
Un bouddha couché de la dynastie Song et des boiseries ouvragées déco-rent le salon du clubhouse.

PAGE DE GAUCHE, EN BAS :
Le salon du clubhouse sert un thé précieux cultivé sur la plantation du Fuchun Resort.

À DROITE, EN HAUT :
La salle à manger, avec son haut plafond, ses boiseries et ses poutres apparentes.

À DROITE, EN BAS :
Un coin salon dans l'une des luxueuses villas privées.

FUCHUN RESORT / HANGZHOU

LEFT ABOVE:
Sunlight falling through tall, narrow, wood-latticed windows lends a meditative mood to the swimming pool area.

LEFT BELOW:
Serving the region's famous "Longjing", or "Dragon Well," tea, one of the finest green teas in China.

RIGHT ABOVE:
Each private villa has its own swimming pool.

RIGHT BELOW:
Another view of a private swimming pool. Each villa also has four bedrooms.

LINKS OBEN:
Das Sonnenlicht, das im Poolbereich durch die hohen, schmalen holzgerahmten Fenster dringt, schafft eine besinnliche Stimmung.

LINKS UNTEN:
Der berühmte „Longjing" oder „Dragon Well" ist einer der besten Grüntees Chinas.

RECHTE SEITE OBEN:
Swimmingpool in einer der Privatvillen.

RECHTE SEITE UNTEN:
Jede Privatvilla verfügt über vier Schlafzimmer und einen eigenen Pool.

À GAUCHE, EN HAUT :
Les hautes fenêtres étroites et treillissées laissent filtrer une lumière méditative sur la piscine.

À GAUCHE, EN BAS :
Le célèbre « Longjing » de la région, ou « puits du Dragon », est un des meilleurs thés verts de Chine.

PAGE DE DROITE, EN HAUT :
Chaque villa privée à sa propre piscine.

PAGE DE DROITE, EN BAS :
Une autre vue de la piscine. Chaque villa compte quatre chambres à coucher.

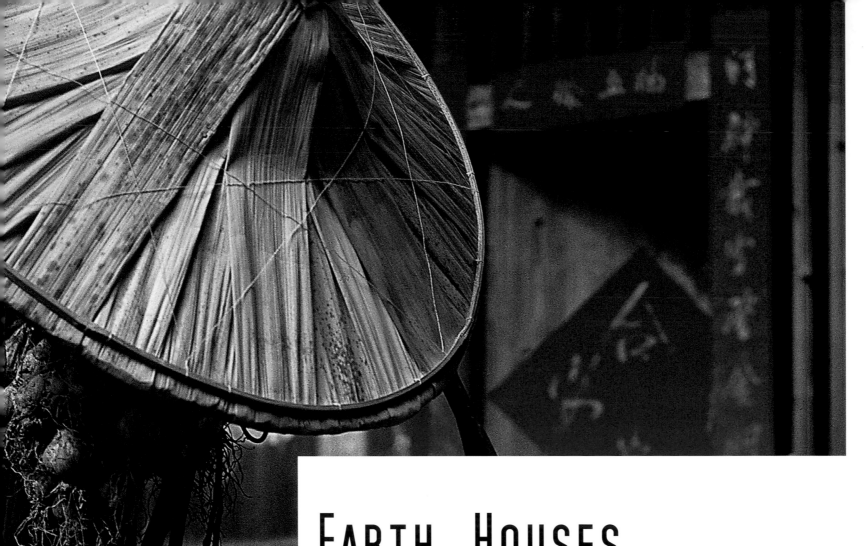

EARTH HOUSES

FUJIAN

The Hakka people migrated south from the mountains of Central China more than 1,500 years ago. Settling far from their origins, they were treated as strangers and sometimes pariahs (the word *Hakka* in Chinese means "guest families"). For centuries they lived inside fortified walls, and preserved their unique language and culture. The Round Earth Houses of Fujian Province are not only an extraordinary architectural legacy, the *tu lou* dwelling complexes also protected the Hakka people from attack.

Some of the Earth Houses have been standing for 600 years. The three to five story multi-family structures, each of which can house between 200 and 400 families, are like an ancient version of an urban apartment complex. The rammed-earth construction material is not only cheap and functional – it is also 100 percent recyclable. The Earth Houses, with their geometric forms set against the green Fujian Mountains, make for a spectacular sight. No wonder Japanese researchers once called them "Black UFOs." In the 1960s, the CIA even sent an agent here to investigate the "suspicious Chinese nuclear plant" he saw in the satellite photograph.

PREVIOUS DOUBLE PAGE:
The Tianluokeng complex of Earth Houses is located in a spectacularly scenic terraced valley in Nanjing County, Fujian. The complex, built between 1796 and 1966, is a listed historic village. One hundred and five families from the Huang clan still live here.

LEFT PAGE:
Detail of the first-floor entry to a dwelling, Tianluokeng.

LEFT:
A round house at Tianluokeng. The exterior windows of the Earth Houses are small, originally to protect its inhabitants from attack.

VORIGE DOPPELSEITE:
Die historischen Erdhäuser von Tianluokeng liegen in einem terrassierten Tal im Bezirk Nanjing der Provinz Fujian. Sie wurden zwischen 1796 und 1966 gebaut und stehen unter Denkmalschutz. Heute leben hier noch 105 Familien des Huang Clan.

LINKE SEITE:
Eingang im ersten Geschoss eines der Häuser von Tianluokeng.

LINKS:
Die Außenfenster der runden Tianluokeng-Erdhäuser wurden sehr klein gebaut, um die Häuser besser vor Angriffen zu schützen.

DOUBLE PAGE PRÉCÉDENTE :
Le complexe de maisons rondes de Tianluokeng est situé dans une vallée en terrasses spectaculaire dans le comté de Nanjing, dans le Fujian. Construit entre 1796 et 1966, c'est un village historique géré par le gouvernement. 105 familles du clan Huang y vivent encore.

PAGE DE GAUCHE :
Détail d'une porte d'entrée au premier étage d'une habitation de Tianluokeng.

À GAUCHE :
Une maison ronde de Tianluokeng. Les fenêtres donnant sur l'extérieur de la structure sont petites pour prévenir les attaques.

Vor mehr als 1500 Jahren wanderten die Hakka vom Norden über die Berge Zentralchinas in den Süden ein, genauer in die Provinz Fujian. Dort lebten sie jahrhundertelang als Außenseiter und Geächtete. Zeugen dieser Isolation sind ihre runden Erdhäuser, die *tu lou*. Sie dienten als Schutz vor Banditen, Feinden, wilden Tieren und gehören zu den Besonderheiten Chinas. Mittlerweile ist eine Anerkennung als UNESCO-Weltkulturerbe beantragt.

Obschon einige dieser Erdhäuser 600 Jahre alt sind, stellen sie moderne und urbane Wohnsiedlungen dar. Als drei- bis fünfgeschossige Mehrfamilienhäuser bieten sie Platz für 200 bis 400 Familien. Gebaut sind sie aus gestampfter Erde, einem billigen Baumaterial, das zu 100 Prozent wiederverwertbar, im Winter warm und im Sommer kühl ist. Die spektakulären, außerirdisch wirkenden Erdhäuser am Fuß der grünen, terrassierten Berge von Fujian wurden nicht von ungefähr von Forschern aus Japan „Schwarze UFOs" genannt. Und in den 1960ern untersuchte sogar ein CIA-Agent die Siedlung, nachdem sie als „verdächtige Nuklearanlage" auf einem Satellitenfoto entdeckt worden waren.

Les Hakkas sont descendus des montagnes du centre il y a plus de 1500 ans. Fixés loin de leur terre d'origine, ils furent traités en étrangers, parfois en parias (*Hakka* signifie « familles invitées »). Pendant des siècles, dans leurs forteresses, ils ont formé un peuple à part, préservant leur langue et leur culture. Leurs *tu lou* ronds constituent le legs architectural de leurs luttes millénaires. En voie d'inscription au patrimoine mondial par l'UNESCO, ils les ont protégés des ennemis et des animaux sauvages.

Certains ont 600 ans mais leur concept architectural est parfaitement en accord avec les styles et préoccupations actuels. Les structures de 3 à 5 étages accueillent entre 200 et 400 familles et rappellent nos HLM. La terre battue avec laquelle elles sont bâties est bon marché, fonctionnelle, chaude l'hiver, fraîche l'été et écologique. Se dressant sur les terrasses des monts Fujian, elles offrent un spectacle superbe, quasi irréel. Des chercheurs japonais les ont pris pour des « OVNIs noirs ». Dans les années 1960, la CIA a même enquêté sur cette « centrale nucléaire suspecte » repérée par satellite.

LEFT ABOVE:
Earth Houses at Tianluokeng. This complex consists of one square, one oval, and three round buildings. From above, the complex is said to resemble a plum blossom.

LEFT BELOW:
Inside the courtyard of a Round Earth House at Tianloukeng. The floors are made of stone, and the staircases and columns are built of wood. Walls are made of rammed earth strengthened with lime, sand, rice, and bamboo.

RIGHT ABOVE:
The interior courtyard is used for cooking and communal dining. Pigs and chickens are housed in the outbuildings.

RIGHT BELOW:
Nowadays, the Earth Houses are inhabited mainly by elderly Hakka villagers. People are moving away from the Earth Houses, to China's modernized cities

LINKE SEITE OBEN:
Tianluokeng besteht aus drei runden Häusern, einem ovalen Haus und einem rechteckigen. Aus der Vogelperspektive sieht die Anlage wie eine Pflaumenblüte aus.

LINKE SEITE UNTEN:
Der Innenhof eines der runden Erdhäuser mit Steinböden, Holztreppen und -pfosten. Die Mauern aus gestampfter Erde wurden mit Kalk, Sand, Reis und Bambus verstärkt.

RECHTS OBEN:
Im Innenhof wird gekocht und gemeinsam gegessen. Schweine und Hühner sind in einem Nebengebäude untergebracht.

RECHTS UNTEN:
Die Erdhäuser werden heute vor allem von älteren Hakka bewohnt. Immer mehr Bewohner ziehen weg, um sich in den modernen Städten Chinas niederzulassen.

PAGE DE GAUCHE, EN HAUT :
Les maisons en terre de Tianluokeng. Le complexe en compte trois rondes, une ovale et une carrée. Vu de haut, l'ensemble rappellerait des fleurs de prunier.

PAGE DE GAUCHE, EN BAS :
L'intérieur de la cour d'une maison ronde. Les sols sont en pierres les escaliers et les colonnes en bois. Les murs sont en terre compactée et renforcée avec de la chaux, du sable, du riz et des bambous.

À DROITE, EN HAUT :
La cour intérieure sert pour la cuisine et les repas communautaires. Les cochons et les poules sont logés dans des bâtiments séparés.

À DROITE, EN BAS :
Aujourd'hui, les tu lou sont principalement habités par des Hakkas âgés. Les gens désertent de plus en plus les maisons en terre au profit des villes modernes

EARTH HOUSES / FUJIAN

LEFT PAGE:
Three generations of a family outside the main entry to a house in the Tianluokeng complex. Some Earth Houses have electricity now, as evidenced by the bulb above.

RIGHT PAGE:
The ground floor of the Earth House is typically used for preparing and eating meals. Each family has its own kitchen. Drying vegetables hang from above.

LINKE SEITE:
Drei Generationen einer Familie vor dem Haupteingang eines Hauses in Tianluokeng. Wie man an der Leuchte oben erkennen kann, sind einige der Erdhäuser ans Stromnetz angeschlossen.

RECHTE SEITE:
Das Erdgeschoss wird hauptsächlich zur Zubereitung von Mahlzeiten genutzt, die hier auch eingenommen werden. Jede Familie verfügt über eine eigene Küche. Vom Geländer im Obergeschoss baumelt getrocknetes Gemüse.

180

PAGE DE GAUCHE :
Trois générations d'une même famille devant l'entrée du complexe de Tianluokeng. Certains tu lou ont désormais l'électricité, comme en témoigne la lampe au-dessus de l'entrée.

PAGE DE DROITE :
C'est généralement au rez-de-chaussée du tu lou qu'on cuisine et qu'on prend ses repas. Chaque habitation possède sa propre cuisine. Des légumes sèchent, accrochés aux poutres du premier étage.

The villagers of the
Tianloukeng Earth House
complex make their living
by farming rice, tea, and
vegetables on the steeply
terraced fields. Their farming methods, and the ter-
races themselves, are
centuries old.

*Die Bewohner der Erdhaus-
siedlung Tianloukeng leben
vom Reis-, Tee- und
Gemüseanbau. Die steil
terrassierten Felder sowie
die Anbautechnik sind
mehrere Jahrhunderte alt.*

*Les villageois du complexe
de Tianloukeng vivent des
champs en terrasse où ils
cultivent du riz, du thé et
des légumes. Leurs métho-
des agricoles, comme les
terrasses elles-mêmes,
sont ancestrales.*

182

LEFT ABOVE:
An ancestral pagoda temple nestled in the green hills at Tianloukeng.

LEFT BELOW:
Women collect water at a stone well inside the walls of a round house at Tianloukeng. Because most people work in the fields, courtyards are empty during the day.

RIGHT ABOVE:
The roofs of the Earth Houses at Tianloukeng are made from gray, locally fired terra-cotta tiles. It takes one year to build a roof.

RIGHT BELOW:
The washing is done by hand at a communal stone well in the Tianluokeng complex.

FOLLOWING DOUBLE PAGE:
The Mazhu Temple in Xiaban Village, Nanjing County, Fujian. In Chinese, the word ma *means mother, and* zhu *means ancestor. In the Hakka culture, families build such elaborate clan houses in honor of their deceased ancestors.*

LINKS OBEN:
Ein Pagodentempel inmitten der grünen Hügel.

LINKS UNTEN:
Frauen schöpfen Wasser aus einem Steinbrunnen im Innenhof eines der Rundhäuser. Tagsüber ist der Innenhof oft leer, da die meisten Bewohner auf dem Feld arbeiten.

RECHTE SEITE OBEN:
Die grauen Dachziegel der Erdhäuser werden vor Ort gebrannt. Es dauert ein Jahr, bis ein Dach fertiggestellt ist.

RECHTE SEITE UNTEN:
In der Tianluokeng-Siedlung wird die Wäsche an einem öffentlichen Brunnen von Hand gewaschen.

FOLGENDE DOPPELSEITE:
Der Mazhu-Tempel von Xiaban im Bezirk Nanjing, Provinz Fujian. Das Wort ma *bedeutet im Chinesischen Mutter und* zhu *Vorfahre. Hakka-Familien bauen solch kunstvolle Gebäude, um ihre Vorfahren zu ehren.*

À GAUCHE, EN HAUT :
Une pagode nichée entre les monts verdoyants à Tianloukeng.

À GAUCHE, EN BAS :
Des femmes puisent l'eau dans un puits à l'intérieur de l'enceinte d'un tu lou. La plupart des habitants travaillant aux champs, les cours sont désertes durant la journée.

PAGE DE DROITE, EN HAUT :
Les toits des tu lou sont en tuiles de terre cuite grises, fabriquées localement. Il faut un an pour achever un toit.

PAGE DE DROITE, EN BAS :
Le linge est lavé à la main au bord du puits communautaire en pierre à l'intérieur du complexe.

DOUBLE PAGE SUIVANTE :
Le temple Mazhu du village de Xiaban, dans le comté de Nanjing, province de Fujian. En chinois ma *signifie « mère » et* zhu*, « ancêtres ». Dans la culture Hakka les familles érigent ces demeures claniques sophistiquées en hommage à leurs ancêtres disparus.*

EARTH HOUSES / FUJIAN

LEFT ABOVE:
Entry to the Yuchang Lou Round Earth House in Xiaban Village, Fujian. The main gate is called "Heaven's Gate."

LEFT BELOW:
A small stone ancestral shrine inside Yuchang Lou. This is one of the oldest Earth Houses, built in 1487.

RIGHT ABOVE:
Yuchang Lou has five stories and 270 rooms. It is famous because its interior wooden columns slant by 15 degrees, giving the building a "drunken" look.

RIGHT BELOW:
Exterior of Yuchang Lou. Like many of the Earth Houses, it is positioned according to Chinese principles of feng shui, with its back to the mountain (yang), facing the water (yin). Many of the Earth Houses are whitewashed to protect the facade against rain, but here it has crumbled away.

LINKS OBEN:
Eingang zum runden Erdhaus Yuchang Lou im Dorf Xiaban in der Provinz Fujian. Das Haupttor heißt „Himmelstor".

LINKS UNTEN:
Yuchang Lou wurde 1487 erbaut und ist eines der ältesten Erdhäuser in Fujian. Hier ein Ahnenschrein aus Stein.

RECHTE SEITE OBEN:
Das Erdhaus Yuchang Lou hat fünf Etagen und 270 Zimmer. Bekannt ist es wegen seiner schiefen Holzsäulen, die das Haus ziemlich wackelig aussehen lassen.

RECHTE SEITE UNTEN:
Wie viele der Erdhäuser ist Yuchang Lou nach den Prinzipien des Feng-Shui angelegt. Es liegt am Wasser (yin), während der hintere Teil den Bergen zugewandt ist (yang). Viele dieser Erdhäuser wurden, um sie vor Regen zu schützen, weiß gekalkt. Hier an der Fassade von Yuchang Lou ist der Kalk im Laufe der Zeit verschwunden.

À GAUCHE, EN HAUT :
L'entrée du Yuchang Lou, dans le village de Xiaban, province de Fujian. Le portail principal s'appelle « la porte du paradis ».

À GAUCHE, EN BAS :
Un petit autel en pierre à l'intérieur du Yuchang Lou. Construit vers 1487, c'est l'un des complexes en terre les plus anciens.

PAGE DE DROITE, EN HAUT :
Yuchang Lou compte trois étages et 270 pièces. Il est célèbre pour ses colonnes en bois inclinées à 15° qui lui donnent l'air « ivre ».

PAGE DE DROITE, EN BAS :
L'extérieur du Yuchang Lou. Comme beaucoup de tu lou, son emplacement répond aux principes chinois du feng shui : tournant le dos à la montagne (yang), face à l'eau (yin). Beaucoup de tu lou sont enduits de chaux pour les protéger contre la pluie mais, ici, elle s'est effritée.

A grand view of all five floors of Yuchang Lou. The building is 18.4 meters high and 54 meters in diameter. The top two floors are used for storage. The second and third are living quarters, and the ground floor is occupied by kitchens. Each floor has 54 rooms, and takes about a year to construct.

Blick auf alle fünf Etagen von Yuchang Lou. Das Haus ist 18,4 Meter hoch und hat einen Durchmesser von 54 Meter. Die beiden oberen Etagen dienen als Speicherraum, in der zweiten und dritten befinden sich die Wohnräume und im Erdgeschoss die Küchen. Jede Etage hat 54 Zimmer. Der Bau einer Etage dauert etwa ein Jahr.

Une belle vue sur les cinq étages de Yuchang Lou, avec ses 18,4 mètres de hauteur et ses 54 mètres de diamètre. Les deux derniers étages servent d'entrepôt ; on vit au premier et au second ; le rez-de-chaussée accueille les cuisines. Chaque étage possède 54 pièces. Il faut environ un an pour le construire.

190

LEFT PAGE:
A close look at a kitchen in Yuchang Lou. The built-in iron wok is fired by a wood stove.

RIGHT PAGE:
Outside the kitchen is a more "modern" stove covered with inexpensive factory-made tiles. The Chinese characters for "double happiness" suggest it was a wedding gift.

LINKE SEITE:
Ein Blick in eine der Küchen von Yuchang Lou. Der eingebaute Wok wird von einem Holzherd befeuert.

RECHTE SEITE:
Vor der Küche steht ein etwas modernerer, mit billigen Fabrikfliesen verkleideter Herd. Die chinesischen Schriftzeichen darauf bedeuten „Doppeltes Glück". Wahrscheinlich handelte es sich dabei um ein Hochzeitsgeschenk.

PAGE DE GAUCHE :
Gros plan sur une cuisine de Yuchang Lou. Le wok encastré est chauffé par un four à bois.

PAGE DE DROITE :
Devant la cuisine, une cuisinière plus « moderne » tapissée de carreaux industriels bon marché. Les symboles du « double bonheur » laissent deviner qu'il s'agit d'un cadeau de mariage.

192

LEFT ABOVE:
In the middle of the courtyard is a small temple. Yuchang Lou's five family clans worship here, burning offerings of incense sticks.

LEFT BELOW:
The fourth floor of the Round Earth House Yuchang Lou. The doors are painted in bright blue to welcome a newly married couple.

RIGHT ABOVE:
Water buffaloes pull plows across the fields. The villagers grow rice and vegetables for their own consumption, and orchids flowers and tea as cash crops.

RIGHT BELOW:
At Yuchang Lou, water is collected in wooden buckets, and the stone floors swept daily with traditional reed brooms.

FOLLOWING DOUBLE PAGE:
Rice terraces reflect late afternoon light near the Yuchang Lou Round Earth House. The fertile, sedimentary earth is the life source of the Hakka people, it is used to build the Earth Houses, and it supports their productive farming.

LINKE SEITE OBEN:
Ein kleiner Tempel mitten im Innenhof. Hier beten die fünf Clans von Yuchang Lou die Götter an und verbrennen Räucherstäbchen, die sie ihnen als Opfer darreichen.

LINKE SEITE UNTEN:
Die vierte Etage von Yuchang Lou. Die Türen wurden für ein frisch vermähltes Paar, das hier einzog, leuchtend blau gestrichen.

RECHTS OBEN:
Wasserbüffel pflügen die Felder. Reis und Gemüse werden von den Dorfbewohnern für den Eigenbedarf angebaut, Orchideen und Tee werden dagegen verkauft.

RECHTS UNTEN:
In Yuchang Lou wird das Wasser in Holzeimern gesammelt, und die Steinböden werden täglich mit traditionellen Schiltbesen gefegt.

FOLGENDE DOPPELSEITE:
Reisterrassen in der Nähe von Yuchang Lou im frühen Abendlicht. Die reiche, sedimentäre Erde ist die Lebensgrundlage der Hakkas. Sie wird sowohl zum Bau der Erdhäuser als auch zum Feldanbau benutzt.

PAGE DE GAUCHE, EN HAUT :
Un petit temple se dresse au milieu de la cour. Les cinq clans de Yuchang Lou viennent y prier, faisant brûler des bâtons d'encens en guise d'offrandes.

PAGE DE GAUCHE, EN BAS :
Le quatrième étage du tu lou. Les portes sont peintes en bleu vif pour accueillir de jeunes mariés.

À DROITE, EN HAUT :
Des buffles tirent une charrue dans un champ. Les villageois cultivent le riz et des légumes pour leur propre consommation, ainsi que des orchidées et du thé destinés à la vente.

À DROITE, EN BAS :
À Yuchang Lou, l'eau est acheminée dans des seaux en bois et les pierres de la cour sont balayées quotidiennement avec des balais traditionnels en joncs.

DOUBLE PAGE SUIVANTE :
Les rizières en terrasse reflètent la lumière de l'après-midi près du complexe rond de Yuchang Lou. La terre riche et sédimentaire est une source vitale pour ces Hakkas. Elle leur sert à construire leurs maisons et leur assure des récoltes généreuses.

195

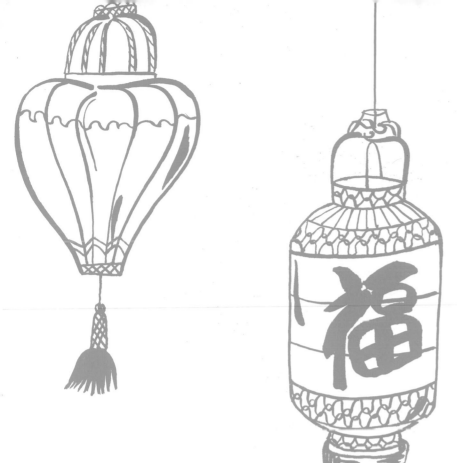

To stay informed about upcoming
TASCHEN titles, please request our magazine at
www.taschen.com/magazine or write to TASCHEN,
Hohenzollernring 53, D–50672 Cologne, Germany,
contact@taschen.com, Fax: +49-221-254919. We
will be happy to send you a copy of our magazine which
is filled with information about all of our books.

Concept, edited and layout by
Angelika Taschen, Berlin
General Project Management by
Stephanie Bischoff, Cologne
Designed by dieSachbearbeiter.innen, Berlin
German translation by Simone Ott Caduff, California
French translation by Philippe Safavi, Paris
Lithography by Thomas Grell, Cologne
Illustrations by Olaf Hajek, www.olafhajek.com

Printed in Germany

ISBN 978-3-8228-4275-1
(Edition with English / German cover)
ISBN 978-3-8365-0240-5
(Edition with French cover)

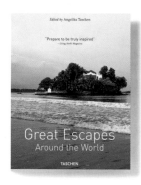

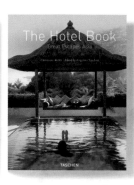

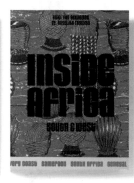
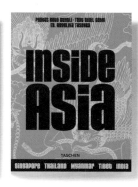
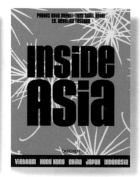
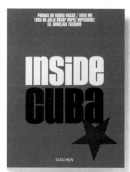

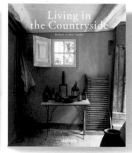

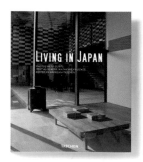

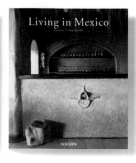
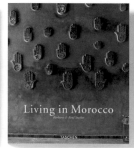

IN PREPARATION
GREAT ESCAPES GERMANY
LIVING IN ARGENTINA